Norma Miller

The Halogen Oven Secret

Also in this Series

The New Curry Secret
The Slow Cooker Secret

Acknowledgements

The recipes in this book were developed using
a range of halogen ovens. In particular,
I would like to thank:

Andrew James UK Ltd.
www.andrewjamesworldwide.com
Tel: 0844 335 8464

Coopers of Stortford.
www.coopersofstortford.co.uk.
Tel: 0844 482 4400

JML Ltd.
www.JMLdirect.com.
Tel: 020 7691 3800

NORMA MILLER

THE HALOGEN OVEN SECRET

RIGHT WAY

Constable & Robinson Ltd
55-56 Russell Square
London WC1B 4HP

www.constablerobinson.com

First published by Right Way, an imprint of Constable & Robinson Ltd, 2010

This illustrated edition published by Right Way, an imprint of Constable & Robinson Ltd, 2011

A copy of the British Library Cataloguing in Publication Data is available from the British Library

ISBN 978-0-71602-303-6

Printed and bound in China

10 9 8 7 6 5 4 3 2 1

Designed by: www.basementpress.com

Pictures Credits

www.shutterstock.com p.24 © Eva Gruendemann, p.27 © Natalia Lisovskaya, p.28 © Martin Turzak, p.33 © Anna Hoychuk, p.41 © Dream79, p.49 © Eva Gruendemann, p.53 © margouillat photo, p.54 © keko64, p.59 © unknown1861, p.62 © PHB.cz (Richard Semik), p.65 © Tristanbm, p.66 © Anatema, p.74 © Patty Orly, p.84 © ep_stock, p.86 © Adrian Britton, p.96 © Olinchuk, p.105 © ivylingpy, p.114 © Joe Gough, p.124 © Monkey Business Images, p.130 © Martin Turzak, p.134 © Quayside, p.147 © Elena Itsenko, p.157 © Monika Wisniewska, p.160 © Vladimira, p.168 © Antonino D'Anna, p.178 © margouillat photo, p.183 © bogumil, p.187 © Giovanna - ricordi fotografici

www.istockphoto.com p.36 © Christina Norwood, p42 © dirkr, p46 © travellinglight, p71 © John Peacock, p89 © Juanmonino, p100 © kantapat, p.118 © Tea Potocnik, p.172 © Robert Anthony

www.alamy.com p.6 © Roger Fletcher, p.80 © Bon Appetit, p.92 © Simon Reddy, p.99 © numb, p.110 © Photocuisine, p.113 © Bon Appetit, p.121 © dk, p.126 © Keith Leighton, p.142 © Bon Appetit, p.151 © UpperCut Images, p.153 © Photocuisine, p.167 © Pick and Mix Images

Contents

WARNING

⚠ 1 Do not touch glass bowl when in use.

2 Never immerse the lid when cleaning,
use damp cloth only

3 Do not attempt to wash bowl or lid when hot.

POWER   HEAT

INTRODUCTION

Halogen ovens have made a rapid rise to popularity. This has been helped by their increasing availability on the high street, by press coverage, by word-of-mouth recommendations, and, perhaps more than anything else, by way of the internet and the opportunity of shopping online. And once you have started using your halogen oven it is easy to understand what makes them so widely appreciated.

Worth a mention

When you have unpacked your halogen oven and read the manufacturer's instruction leaflets, I suggest that the first thing you cook with your new oven is a piece of toast. There is quite a variation between the different models on the market, and this will give you an insight into how your own halogen oven can be handled.

Put a slice of ordinary white toasting bread on the high rack, turn the temperature dial to 250°C and set the timer to around three minutes. This is a way of getting used to handling the equipment, and also you will be able to see how quickly the toast cooks. How even is the browning? Has it toasted on both sides? Does it need turning?

Remember, if you are new to halogen oven cooking, it can be fast.

THE HALOGEN OVEN – WHAT IS IT?

This portable, multi-purpose, table-top oven uses technology that enables food to be cooked using infrared waves from a halogen light source. It cooks up to about 40 per cent faster than a conventional oven, so uses less power and is therefore very economical to run. Halogen ovens will roast, grill, defrost, bake and steam. Conveniently, they just need to be plugged into an earthed mains power socket.

The halogen oven consists of a large glass bowl which rests on a plastic base. The workings are all in the lid which sits on top of the glass bowl. There are two racks: a high rack and a low rack. You can put your food directly onto either of the racks, and each rack can also support dishes and trays.

The lid has a handle which must be used to lift the lid when taking it off or placing it on the glass bowl. The handle also acts as a safety switch; as soon as it is lifted up the machine will turn off. The handle must be flat down for the oven to work – it is very easy at first to forget to push it down flat. There are two control switches. One switch is for the temperature, ranging from 20°C to 250°C. The other control switch is for the time. Select the time by turning the switch in a clockwise direction from 0 to 60 minutes. The halogen oven will not work until the time has been selected. **Important – the timer switch should not be turned backwards as it could damage the halogen oven.** When the oven is switched off, the timer will continue to run and will just tick down back to zero. The halogen light will turn off when it has reached the desired temperature, and then will turn on again when it needs to come back up to the correct temperature. There is also noise from the motor and the hot air circulating.

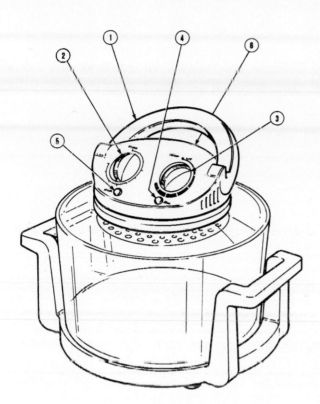

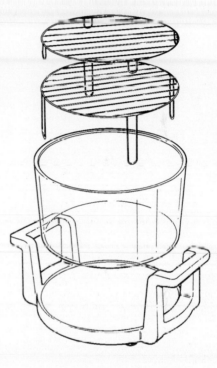

Fig. 1 The halogen oven

1. Handle
2. Time control switch
3. Temperature control switch
4. Green heat light
5. Red power light
6. Safety switch

Fig. 2

Tongs,
low cooking rack,
high cooking rack,
glass bowl
and plastic base

Advantages and limitations

Advantages

- Because the halogen oven uses half the electricity of a conventional oven and about the same as a microwave oven it is very economical.

- It is easy to use – just plug into a 13 amp earthed mains power socket.

- Generally cooking times are shorter. It cooks about 20 per cent faster than a conventional oven on average.

- It is compact and so uses less energy to heat up and so less electricity.

- It is very versatile and allows you to roast, bake, steam, reheat or defrost.

- Foods, especially meat and fish, remain very juicy and moist.

- You can watch your food cooking through the glass bowl.

- For the health conscious, if you choose to cook meats directly on the rack, any fat will drop to the bottom of the oven to be discarded.

Limitations

- The size of the machines may be too small for the number you want to cater for.

- The hot air circulation causes liquids to swirl round, so it's not ideal for soups or very liquid dishes. And they would have to be covered.

- Some vegetables don't cook more quickly than in a conventional oven, so you have to take this into consideration when planning your cooking.

- Rice, pasta, grains and beans are best used pre-cooked, either cooked on the hob whilst you prepare the rest of the dish, or use canned or frozen.

Choosing a halogen oven

Points to consider when buying a halogen oven:

- Look at the models available and find out as much as you can. You will find lots of information.
- How will you use the halogen oven? Will it be used alongside your regular kitchen equipment, the oven and the hob and microwave? Or will it be used as a replacement for your oven? Maybe you will use it on holiday, in a caravan or self-catering apartments, or in student accommodation.
- It is portable so it can be used at home or at work, or you can take it with you when you travel on holiday.
- How much do you want to spend?
- Where will the halogen oven sit? The cord from the oven to the socket is not very long, so where will you be able to put it? There has to be space around it, including space to put down the lid.
- Do you want a halogen oven which offers extra accessories?
- How many people do you cook for – one, two or more? Complete meals can be made for one to three people. For four or more, part of a meal can be prepared, such as a chicken and some of the vegetables, so use your halogen oven alongside your regular equipment.
- Look at the extra accessories available. The extension ring allows larger food to be cooked.
- You may prefer a halogen oven with the option of a 'steamer' rack or toast rack.

Cookware and equipment to use with a halogen oven

- The halogen oven usually comes with both a high and low rack and tongs as standard (see page 9). Other accessories are available and vary with each model of halogen oven, such as a lid-rest (see below).

- In addition, and depending on the type of cooking you do, it is useful to have a range of ovenproof pans, roasting tins, bowls, plates, casserole dishes and flan dishes which will fit into your halogen oven. The types you would use in your ordinary oven will be fine.

- Remember, there must be good clearance around any cooking vessels you place inside your halogen oven to allow the hot air to circulate. I like to use clear glass dishes so that I can see the food inside.

- Foil is useful to cover dishes and can also be used to make 'parcels' in which ingredients can be baked, roasted or steamed. It can also be used as a tray to prevent food from dropping through the bars of the racks.

- A pair of gauntlet-style oven gloves is essential, and also a couple of pairs of different shaped tongs to move the food around.

Fig. 3
Lid-rest supplied by some manufacturers.

Tips for using the halogen oven

- Never leave the machine unattended when it is in use.

- Don't turn the timer backwards as it can damage the machine.

- Cooking with a halogen oven is rather topsy-turvy. A rare steak will cook in about 10 minutes, but if you want a quarter of an onion cooked with it, the onion will take 60 minutes to cook. Once you can grasp this idea you should easily adjust to the expectation that vegetables will take longer to cook than chops, steaks or fish fillets. Firmer vegetables just need to go into the halogen oven earlier. Think ahead.

- Sometimes the side of the food closer to the heat source will brown more quickly, so you may have to turn the food.

- Cooking directly on the racks means the bowl will have to be washed after every use. If you prefer, cook in ovenproof dishes or on trays; the glass bowl will then only need wiping.

- Keep an eye on the food at regular intervals.

- Just cover dishes if they appear to be cooking too quickly.

- The movement of the hot air can cause small light ingredients, such as chopped or whole herb leaves, to move. Make sure they are pushed down under the other ingredients, or for something such as a home-made pizza, turn one of the racks upside-down and rest it on top of the food.

- Foil is useful to cover dishes, and can be used to make 'parcels' in which ingredients can be baked, roasted or steamed. It can also be used as a tray to prevent food from dropping through the bars of the racks.

- When the cooking time has finished, remove the food immediately because moisture will build up in the oven if food is left inside with no heat on. Just turn the temperature dial to 100°C for a few minutes if you need to delay serving the meal.

- Experiment.

Steaming vegetables and fish
- Put prepared vegetables or fish onto a large piece of foil or in an ovenproof dish. Add 1–2 tbsp water, stock or lemon juice, and either gather up the foil and seal the parcel securely, or cover the dish tightly in foil.

Roasting meat or fish
- Brush meat or fish with a little oil, add a few herbs and put directly onto the rack or into a roasting tin.

Baking cakes and scones
- Cook for a shorter time than in a conventional oven, and for fruit cakes reduce the temperature.

Defrosting
- Turn the dial to the 'defrost' or 'thaw' setting.
- For small items such as pastries and rolls set the timer to 5 minutes and keep checking regularly. For larger items such as meat or shop-bought prepared dishes set the timer to 10 minutes and keep checking regularly. Make sure the food is completely thawed – if necessary, add extra time until you are sure.

Care and cleaning

- Read the 'important safety advice section' on the next page.

- Always unplug the halogen oven before cleaning.

- Leave the halogen oven to cool when you have finished cooking in it. If cold water is poured on the glass while it is still hot, it could crack or break the glass.

- The heating element is delicate, so take care not to damage it.

- Remove any food and drain away any grease from the glass bowl.

- The halogen oven has a self-cleaning 'wash' setting.

- To clean the halogen oven, put 5–15cm/2–6 inches of cold water in the bottom of the glass bowl and set the temperature to 100°C and the timer to 10–15 minutes (refer to the manufacturer's instruction booklet).

- Do not get any water in the lid.

- For a dirty oven, add a little mild detergent to the water and use a washing up brush to remove any stubborn stains.

- Do not use any abrasive cleaners or scouring pads in the halogen oven.

- The cooking racks can be left in the glass bowl when cleaning. Any bits of food stuck to the bars will soften.

- Rinse the bowl to remove any detergent and dry.

Important safety advice

Much of this advice should be common sense when using any kitchen appliance:

- The halogen oven must be on a stable heat-proof surface and not near the edge of work surfaces.

- Keep the surrounding areas clear and free from clutter.

- Ensure there is adequate air space around the halogen oven for air to circulate.

- The halogen oven must be plugged into an earthed mains power socket (the red power light will be illuminated).

- Do not operate the halogen oven with other major appliances plugged into the same power socket – there is a risk of fusing the circuit.

- Only use the halogen oven indoors.

- Don't stare directly into the bulb.

- Don't move the halogen oven when in use.

- Don't leave the halogen oven unattended whilst in use.

- Make sure the power cord is not touching anything hot.

- You should always wear oven gloves when handling the hot oven, the racks, dishes, trays and the hot food.

- Do not leave oven gloves or tea towels flopped over the halogen oven.

- Always use ovenproof pans, roasting tins, bowls, plates, casserole dishes and flan dishes which will fit in your halogen oven.

- Do not use paper or plastic in your halogen oven.

- Do not try to turn the timer backwards, as it can damage the machine.

- Before starting to cook in the halogen oven, make sure the lid is securely on top of the oven.

- Ensure there is space around the halogen oven to put the lid down safely on its own stand (if using a stand) or on a heat-proof surface.

- Always use the handle to remove the glass lid from the bowl.

- If you do not have a lid-rest, the lid must be placed on its side on a heat-proof surface.

- Never pick up the hot lid without using oven gloves.

- Before putting the lid on the lid-rest, make sure the halogen oven is unplugged and switched off.

- If you have a lid-rest, make sure it is on a flat, heat proof surface and away from the edge of work surfaces. The lid-rest will get hot after use. The surface must be flat because the lid and lid-rest can easily topple over on an irregular surface.

- Keep children and pets away from the halogen oven when in use.

- Don't immerse the glass lid, power cord or electric plug in hot water or place in a dishwasher.

- All parts of the halogen oven must be dry before using.

- Don't put the halogen oven on a cooker hob or in the oven.

- Don't put the oven away until it is cold.

- If any faults occur with your halogen oven always contact the manufacturer.

About the recipes

- All the recipes have been designed specifically for cooking in a halogen oven, and the preparation and cooking processes for each recipe are straightforward and easy to follow. To make things even easier, there are plenty of serving suggestions and hints and tips to go with the recipes.

- Mostly the recipes serve two, three or four people. They use a mixture of fresh seasonal produce, store-cupboard ingredients and canned foods, as well as some frozen items. The recipes are often adaptable, and you can easily substitute interchangeable ingredients as you wish. For example, I like chopping and slicing fresh chillies, ginger, garlic and herbs, but do use pastes and purées if you prefer.

- For convenience, the recipe ingredients are listed in the order in which they are used. Though they are given in imperial as well as metric, you will find the metric measurements easier.

- Some of the recipes can produce extra servings by doubling the quantities of ingredients – but make sure this increased volume still goes into your halogen oven. Or you can make a smaller amount by scaling down the quantities.

- Is your halogen oven large enough? Think about the size and capacity of your oven when buying joints of meat or whole fish. Indeed, this applies equally to the number of servings and the size of the food you want to make – sliced vegetables take up a much larger space than when left whole and six large jacket potatoes probably won't fit in the oven on one rack.

- At the start of each recipe there is an instruction to pre-heat the oven. Check with your instruction book for the recommended times and pre-heat accordingly. Food can be put into a cold oven, but pre-heating reduces the cooking time a little.

- Also at the start of each recipe there is a mention of the type of cooking equipment you will need such as 'ovenproof dish', 'roasting tin' or 'tray'. These are then referred to in the method as the dish, the roasting tin or the tray.

- Cooking times are always approximate. Halogen ovens do differ in their performance from model to model. Ingredients vary in their quality, shape, size and temperature (room temperature or fridge-cold, and so on).

- Where a recipe calls for boiling water, I have used a kettle and then added the boiling water to the recipe. This not only saves time but can save energy too.

- Please don't simply rely on cooking times. Always use conventional methods of checking that food is cooked. Is it tender, soft, cooked through, thickened, bubbling, piping hot? Do the juices of the meat and poultry run clear? Can the fish be separated into flakes? Are the vegetables tender? And are the cakes cooked in the centre? Or think of using a cooking thermometer.

- When a recipe needs stirring, turning or covering, instructions are given.

- Do take into account whether your oven browns quickly or not; you may need to reduce or increase the temperature by a few degrees or reduce or increase the cooking time.

- You can of course brown ingredients in a pan on the hob, or for casserole-style recipes ingredients can be brought up to the boil before putting into a suitable dish for the halogen oven. The cooking times will then be reduced.

- I find it is preferable to use pre-cooked varieties of rice, beans, pasta and noodles.

- The recipes have been tested with a variety of halogen ovens.

- My store-cupboard always contains canned tomatoes, a selection of canned beans, and small jars of pastes that are so quick and convenient – garlic, curry and chilli. Also a wide selection of spices and spice mixes. I prefer to use fresh herbs if possible. I also find it is useful to keep frozen peas and bags of mixed seafood in the freezer.

- Another favourite store-cupboard ingredient is liquid concentrated stock or vegetable bouillon powder. I particularly like using this because it is granular, and you can spoon out as much or as little as you want.

- All spoon measures are level unless otherwise stated.

- Salt is kept to a minimum. Instead I prefer to source good quality ingredients that have bags of flavour. Often just a handful of freshly chopped herbs is all you need to boost flavour. Salt is included in some of the recipes, but use with discretion.

- Some recipes contain eggs – please remember that it may be advisable to avoid eating eggs if you are pregnant, elderly, very young or sick.

- If you are preparing food for someone who has a food allergy be sure to study the list of ingredients carefully.

- Some recipes contain fresh chillies. Do take care when preparing them and remember to wash your hands thoroughly afterwards. Better still, wear rubber gloves while handling them.

Cooking times

These cooking times are only a guide. Always ensure the food is piping hot and cooked through before serving.

Timings will always vary because of the shape and thickness of the food to be cooked. Timings can be found in all the recipes in this book.

Roast Beef
1kg/2 lb 3½ oz: 190°C–200°C about 65–75 minutes – low rack

Steak
175g/6 oz: 200°C about 8–10 minutes for rare, 12–15 minutes for medium and 12–18 minutes for well done – high rack

Sausages
200°C about 12–15 minutes – high rack

Bacon rashers
200°C about 10–12 minutes – high rack

Chicken
1.3kg/3 lb: 190°C–200°C about 60–75 minutes – low rack

Chicken breast
175g/6 oz: 190°C–200°C about 15–20 minutes – high rack

Fish fillet
140g/5 oz: 200°C about 12–18 minutes – high rack

Jacket potato
225g/8 oz: 200°C about 50–60 minutes – low/high rack

Sweet potato
225g/8 oz: 200°C about 35–45 minutes – low/high rack

Quarter of an onion
200°C about 50–60 minutes – low/high rack

Finely chopped onion
200°C about 25–35 minutes – low/high rack

Peas, sliced peppers, sliced courgettes
200°C about 15–25 minutes – low/high rack

ADAPTING RECIPES FOR THE HALOGEN OVEN

Look at a recipe that you would usually cook on the hob or in a traditional oven. Look at the ingredients, and if there are vegetables which will have a longer cooking time, deal with those first and cook them in the halogen oven first before adding, say, the fish or meat. I have mentioned before that this is a topsy-turvy way of cooking, but the more you practise, the more it will become second nature to think about how to order the cooking. For example, I chop some types of vegetables very finely; they can then be roasted in a little oil before completing the recipe.

So do experiment. Use your usual cooking temperature, but cook for a little less time. If dishes brown too quickly because they are closer to the heat source, cover with a lid or foil, reduce the temperature, or put onto a lower shelf.

1. JUST VEGETABLES

Vegetables are varied and versatile, and very good for you too. These vegetable dishes are ideal for vegetarians and non-vegetarians alike. Whether as substantial snacks or as main meals, they are enticing enough to eat on their own, or maybe with a salad or some bread to accompany them. There is plenty to enjoy here, including Sesame Spiced Potatoes with Cauliflower and Spinach (page 30), Vegetable Tart (page 38) and Green Bean and Green Pepper Thai Curry (page 50).

Some dishes contain cheese, and vegetarians will want to select the vegetarian versions of those particular cheeses. Non-vegetarians can always add a little meat or fish to any of these recipes.

VEGETABLE NIBBLES WITH A CHILLI GINGER DIPPING SAUCE

Roasted vegetables look very colourful as they keep their bright colours. Dunk them into the spicy yogurt dip.

SERVES 4	2 medium carrots	Dipping Sauce
as a snack	2 medium parsnips	400ml/¾ pint Greek yogurt
	2 courgettes	¼ tsp chilli paste
	1 red pepper	¼ tsp garlic paste
	1 green pepper	¼ tsp ginger paste
	2 tbsp sunflower oil	Freshly milled salt and pepper

1   Remove the lid from the halogen oven, place the low rack inside the oven and replace the lid. Preheat the oven to 200°C.

2   Peel the carrots and parsnips and trim the courgettes. Cut them all into finger-sized batons. Cut the red and green peppers in half, remove and discard the seeds and stalks, and cut into slices.

3   Pour the oil into a large bowl. Stir in the batons of carrots and parsnips until lightly coated. Lift out of the bowl and put into the hot oven on the low rack. (They will tumble onto the base of the oven, but that's all right – put them on a tray or foil if you prefer.) Cook for 10–15 minutes until beginning to soften.

4   Stir the batons of courgettes and both red and green peppers into the oil and put into the hot oven with the carrots and parsnips. Cook for 12–20 minutes or until they are cooked through and slightly browned. Timings will depend upon the thickness of the batons. With tongs, remove the cooked vegetables to a bowl. Don't leave in the oven without heat otherwise they will soften. When the vegetable batons are cooked, return to the hot oven for a few minutes to reheat.

5   Pour the yogurt into a bowl, stir in the chilli, garlic and ginger pastes and season to taste. Mix thoroughly and season if necessary. Serve the dip with the vegetable nibbles.

MIXED VEGETABLE SKEWERS

The vegetables can be varied to suit your taste. Serve with soured cream, salad and hot wraps. You will need four metal skewers and a greased baking tray which fits in your oven.

SERVES 2

8 button mushrooms
1 green pepper
1 medium courgette
1 tbsp olive oil
2 tbsp pesto
2 tsp lemon juice

Freshly milled salt and black pepper
8 cherry tomatoes
4 small new potatoes, canned or frozen
4 pickled onions
2 mini corn cobs, frozen

1   Remove the lid from the halogen oven, place the high rack inside the oven and replace the lid. Preheat the oven to 180°C.

2   Trim the mushroom stalks level with the base of the caps. Cut the pepper in half, remove and discard the seeds and stalk, and cut into 8 pieces. Trim the courgette and cut into 8 slices.

3   In a small bowl mix together the olive oil, pesto, lemon juice and a little seasoning.

4   Thread the mushrooms, the pieces of pepper, the slices of courgette, the cherry tomatoes, potatoes, pickled onions and mini corn cobs onto four metal skewers, leaving a small gap between each piece.

5   Brush the skewers with the pesto mixture and put onto the baking tray. Spoon over any remaining mixture.

6   Put into the hot oven and cook for 15–20 minutes, turning once, until roasted, piping and cooked through.

POTATO WEDGES WITH A CRUSHED HERB AND PEANUT COATING

Potato wedges are always a favourite, especially when coated with such a tasty mix. You will need a greased baking tray or roasting tin which fits in your oven.

SERVES 4	¼ tsp fennel seeds	Freshly milled black pepper
	1 tsp dried mixed herbs	450g/1 lb potatoes
	A handful of unsalted peanuts	1 tbsp sunflower oil

1 Remove the lid from the halogen oven, place the low rack inside the oven and replace the lid. Preheat the oven to 200°C.

2 Put the fennel seeds, mixed herbs, peanuts, and a little black pepper into a food (freezer) bag and finely crush with a rolling pin or use a food processor.

3 Peel the potatoes, cut into wedges and put into a large bowl.

4 Pour over the oil and stir until lightly coated.

5 Sprinkle the ground peanut mixture over the oiled potatoes and mix until coated.

6 Arrange the wedges on the tray or roasting tin and put into the hot oven. Cook for 20–35 minutes until browned, piping hot and cooked through.

Choose your favourite filling from the list opposite. You can, of course, add a little chopped cooked meat or fish if you wish.

SERVES 1	1 large jacket potato, about 250g/9 oz
	Oil or butter
	Freshly milled black pepper

1   Remove the lid from the halogen oven, place the low rack inside the oven and replace the lid. Preheat the oven to 200°C.

2   Scrub the potato and dry with kitchen paper. Pierce a few times with a skewer or the point of a sharp knife. Rub a little oil or butter into the skin and wrap in foil.

3   Put into the hot oven and cook for about 40–45 minutes until soft, look after 30 minutes to see if it is piping hot and cooked through.

4   Cut in half, add a little butter and black pepper and serve whilst hot.

5   To add a filling: Cut the potato in half, scoop the soft potato into a bowl. Mix in your chosen filling and spoon back into the potato skins. Return to the oven and cook for 8–12 minutes until piping hot and cooked through.

Fillings *for one potato*

Cheddar Cheese, Mustard and Walnuts
2 tbsp grated Cheddar cheese, 1 tsp mild mustard and a few broken walnuts

Red Pimento, Pine Nuts and Rocket
Chopped red pimento, a few pine nuts and rocket leaves

Garlic, Chilli and Butter and Spinach Leaves
¼ tsp each of garlic and chilli paste, a little butter and a few shredded spinach leaves

Mozzarella Cheese, Black Olives, Oregano and Walnut
Torn mozzarella cheese, 3 stoned black olives, sliced, a few oregano leaves and a few walnut pieces

Curry, Mango Chutney and Tomatoes
¼ tsp curry paste, 1 tbsp mango chutney and 2 chopped tomatoes

Sesame Spiced Potatoes with Cauliflower and Spinach

Serve just as it is, with salad or with roasted fish or meats. You will need a large shallow ovenproof dish which fits in your oven.

SERVES 3–4 as an accompaniment	1 red onion	1 tbsp sesame seeds
	¼ cauliflower	150ml/¼ pint vegetable stock
	300g/10½ oz potatoes	1 tbsp lemon juice
	1 tbsp olive oil	2 large handfuls of spinach leaves
	2 tsp sesame seed oil	Freshly milled salt and black pepper

1 Remove the lid from the halogen oven, place the low rack inside the oven and replace the lid. Preheat the oven to 190°C.

2 Finely chop the onion. Break the cauliflower into small florets. Cut the potatoes into small bite-sized cubes.

3 Pour the olive oil and sesame seed oil into the dish and stir in the onion and sesame seeds.

4 Put the dish into the hot oven and cook for 8–10 minutes until the onion begins to soften and brown. Remove the dish from the oven, replace the lid and set the timer to 40 minutes.

5 Pour the stock and lemon juice into the hot dish and stir in the cubes of potato, cauliflower florets, spinach leaves and a little seasoning.

6 Cover the dish and put back into the hot oven. Cook for 35–45 minutes until piping hot and cooked through, but look after 30 minutes to see if it is ready.

POTATO AND PARSNIP CHEESE AND ONION LAYER

There's a long cooking time for this dish, but it's worth the wait. You will need a large buttered, shallow ovenproof dish which fits in your oven.

SERVES 2-3	250g/9 oz potatoes	100g/3½ oz hard cheese, such as Cheddar or
	250g/9 oz parsnips	pecorino cheese
	1 medium red onion	Freshly milled salt and black pepper
	1 garlic clove	5 tbsp milk
	Large bunch of parsley	50g/1¾ oz butter

1   Remove the lid from the halogen oven, place the low rack inside the oven and replace the lid. Preheat the oven to 200°C.

2   Peel and very thinly slice the potatoes and parsnips. Finely chop the onion and the garlic. Finely chop the parsley and grate the cheese.

3   In the buttered dish, layer the potato and parsnip slices, onion, garlic, parsley and about two-thirds of the cheese, adding a little seasoning as you go. Pour over the milk and scatter over the remaining cheese. Dot the surface with small pieces of the butter.

4   Cover the dish and put into the hot oven. Cook for 60 minutes or until piping hot and cooked through.

Spiced Red Cabbage with Apples and Sultanas

A sweet and sour dish – full of contrasting flavours, and very comforting too. You will need a wide ovenproof dish which fits in your oven.

SERVES 4 as an accompaniment		
¼ red cabbage, about 280g/10 oz	1 tbsp bouillon powder	
1 small red onion	2 tbsp red wine vinegar	
1 garlic clove	2 tbsp clear honey	
2 red eating apples	2 tsp chilli sauce	
1 lime	Handful of sultanas	

1. Remove the lid from the halogen oven, place the low rack inside the oven and replace the lid. Preheat the oven to 200°C.

2. Slice the cabbage in half, remove and discard the central core, and cut into very fine shreds. Cook the cabbage in a pan of boiling water for 12 minutes and drain well.

3. Put the kettle on to boil. Finely chop the onion and crush the garlic. Core and finely chop the apples. Finely grate the rind from the lime, cut in half and squeeze out the juice.

4. Pour 350ml/12 fl oz boiling water (from the kettle) into a jug and stir in the bouillon powder, vinegar, honey, chilli sauce and the lime rind and juice.

5. Tip the drained cabbage into the dish and pour over the stock mixture. Stir in the onion, garlic, apple and sultanas. Cover tightly.

6. Put the dish into the hot oven and cook for 1–1¼ hours until piping hot and cooked through. Look after 50 minutes to see if it is ready.

ROASTED MINI VEGETABLES WITH CHERRY TOMATOES

Mini vegetables are fun to cook with. Mixed trays of them are readily available from stores. You will need foil and a wide shallow ovenproof dish or roasting tin which fits in your oven.

SERVES 4	500g/1 lb 2 oz mixed mini vegetable selection, such as, yellow and green courgettes, red peppers, leeks, carrots and turnips Four sprays of cherry tomatoes, about 2–4 tomatoes on each spray	3 rosemary sprigs 6 sprigs of oregano Olive oil Freshly milled salt and black pepper ½ lemon

1   Remove the lid from the halogen oven, place the low rack inside the oven (you will also use the high rack) and replace the lid. Preheat the oven to 220°C.

2   Trim the vegetables, leaving the leaves intact. If they are large, then cut in half lengthways. Pull the leaves from the rosemary and oregano.

3   Pour 1–2 tbsp of the oil into the dish or tin. Stir in the rosemary and oregano leaves, the mini vegetables and a little seasoning. Squeeze over the lemon juice.

4   Put the dish or tin into the hot oven and cook for 20–30 minutes until the vegetables are beginning to roast.

5   Meanwhile, put a piece of foil on the high rack, arrange the tomatoes on the foil and drizzle with a little oil.

6   After 20–30 minutes, remove the lid from the oven. Put in the high rack and the tomatoes, close the lid and cook for a further 12–15 minutes or until the vegetables have roasted and the tomatoes have softened.

Steamed Vegetables with Hot Lemon Myrtle Dressing

All the lovely flavours of the vegetables are sealed in the foil parcel. You will need foil and a small ovenproof jug or bowl which fits in your oven.

SERVES 2-3

2 carrots	Freshly milled black pepper
2 courgettes	150ml/¼ pint passata, sieved tomatoes
175g/6 oz piece of mooli (white radish or daikon)	1–2 tsp lemon myrtle powder
3 spring onions	1 tbsp chopped parsley
1 tbsp vegetable or chicken bouillon powder	1 tbsp olive oil

1 Remove the lid from the halogen oven, place the low rack inside the oven and replace the lid. Preheat the oven to 220°C.

2 Put the kettle on to boil. Trim and peel the carrots, courgettes and mooli and cut into long thin shreds like shoe laces. Trim the spring onions and finely slice.

3 Pour 300ml/½ pint boiling water (from the kettle) into a jug and stir in the bouillon powder.

4 Put the pieces of carrot, courgette, mooli and spring onions onto the centre of a large piece of foil and pull up the edges. Sprinkle over a little black pepper and spoon over 4 tbsp of the stock. Gather up the edges of the foil and pinch together to make a parcel.

5 Pour the remaining stock into the jug or bowl and stir in the passata, lemon myrtle, chopped parsley, olive oil and a little black pepper. Cover with foil.

6 Put the vegetable parcel and the jug or bowl of dressing into the hot oven and cook for 25–35 minutes or until the vegetables are tender and cooked and the dressing is piping hot.

ROASTED PUMPKIN AND HALLOUMI

Halloumi cheese has a firm texture and is a good partner to pumpkin. Allspice adds the flavours of cinnamon, cloves and nutmeg. You will need a shallow ovenproof dish which fits in your oven.

SERVES 4	500g/1 lb 2 oz piece of pumpkin or squash	1 tbsp olive oil
	200g/7 oz halloumi cheese	2 tsp butter
	2 tbsp clear honey	¼ tsp ground allspice
	1 tbsp lime juice	Freshly milled black pepper

1   Remove the lid from the halogen oven, place the low rack inside the oven and replace the lid. Preheat the oven to 200°C.

2   Peel the pumpkin or squash, scoop out and discard any seeds and cut into bite-sized pieces. Cut the halloumi cheese into slices.

3   Put the honey, lime juice, olive oil and butter into the dish. Put into the oven for 1–2 minutes to warm and melt the honey and butter.

4   Remove the dish from the oven, close the lid and turn the timer to 30 minutes.

5   Stir the allspice and a little black pepper into the honey mixture and then add the pumpkin or squash pieces and slices of halloumi cheese. Carefully turn in the honey mixture until coated and spread them to a single layer. Put the dish into the hot oven and cook for 15–25 minutes, turning once until the pumpkin and halloumi cheese are golden, piping hot and cooked through.

VEGETABLE TART

Rather like a savoury cheese cake in a pastry case. You will need a baking tray which fits in your oven.

SERVES 4

200g/7 oz cooked vegetables, such as artichoke
   hearts, leeks or tiny broad beans
Small handful of taco crisps
2 medium eggs
140g/5 oz low-fat cream cheese

2 tbsp milk
1 tbsp chopped fresh chives
Freshly milled black pepper
20cm/8 inch cooked pastry case

1   Remove the lid from the halogen oven, place the low rack inside the oven and replace the lid. Preheat the oven to 190°C.

2   Slice the vegetables or leave whole and dry on kitchen paper. Crush the taco crisps.

3   Break the eggs into a bowl, add the cream cheese, milk, chives and a little black pepper and beat well.

4   Put the pastry case (still in its foil tray) on the baking tray and arrange the vegetables in the base. Pour the egg mixture over the vegetables and scatter over the crushed tacos.

5   Put the tray into the hot oven and cook for 20–35 minutes until the pastry is cooked and the filling is piping hot and cooked through.

Steamed Roots

The longer cooking times of root vegetables in the halogen oven can be reduced by pre-cooking in boiling water for six to eight minutes. You will need a wide ovenproof dish which fits in your oven.

SERVES 2		
	1 parsnip	1 tbsp liquid chicken or vegetable stock
	1 small white turnip	2 tbsp red wine, optional
	1 carrot	Freshly milled black pepper
	1 small leek	1 bay leaf
	1 shallot	2 sprigs of thyme

1   Remove the lid from the halogen oven, place the low rack inside the oven and replace the lid. Preheat the oven to 190°C.

2   Put the kettle on to boil. Peel and trim the vegetables. Finely chop the parsnip and turnip and thinly slice the carrot and leek. Very finely chop the shallot.

3   Pour 150ml/¼ pint boiling water (from the kettle) into a jug and stir in the liquid stock and wine, if using, or extra water and black pepper.

4   Put the prepared vegetables into the dish and pour over the stock mixture. Push the bay leaf and thyme sprigs under the surface of the liquid.

5   Cover tightly and put the dish into the hot oven. Cook for 45–60 minutes or until the vegetables are tender, piping hot and cooked through.

CURRIED SWEET POTATO WITH COURGETTE AND ONION

Choose whichever flavour of curry paste you like. This dish is almost a meal in itself. You will need a large, buttered, shallow ovenproof dish which fits in your oven.

SERVES 2–3

2 large sweet potatoes, about 250 g/9 oz each
2 courgettes
1 large onion
1 garlic clove
Small bunch of coriander

2–3 tbsp mild curry paste
425 ml/¾ pint chicken or vegetable stock
Freshly milled salt and black pepper
1–2 tbsp olive oil

1   Remove the lid from the halogen oven, place the low rack inside the oven and replace the lid. Preheat the halogen oven to 200°C.

2   Peel and very thinly slice the sweet potatoes and courgettes. Finely chop the onion, garlic and coriander. Stir the curry paste into the stock until well mixed.

3   In the buttered dish, layer the sweet potato and courgette slices, the onion, garlic and coriander, adding a little seasoning as you go. Pour over the flavoured stock and drizzle with a little oil.

4   Cover the dish loosely with foil. Put the dish into the hot oven and cook for 40–50 minutes until piping hot and cooked through.

CUMIN AND CORIANDER AUBERGINE CHUNKS WITH PINE NUTS

The spices give a delicious fragrance to aubergine. Perfect with oily fish or roasted chicken. You will need a large, oiled, shallow ovenproof dish which fits in your oven.

SERVES 2–3	2 aubergines	2 tsp ground cumin
	1 red onion	Freshly milled salt and black pepper
	2 tbsp olive oil	Handful of pine nuts
	2 tsp ground coriander	Lemon wedges

1   Remove the lid from the halogen oven, place the low rack inside the oven and replace the lid. Preheat the halogen oven to 200°C.

2   Trim and discard the aubergine stalks and cut into thick chunks. Very finely chop the onion. In a small bowl, mix together the oil, ground coriander, cumin, chopped onion and a little seasoning.

3   Arrange the aubergine pieces in the dish and pour over the spice mixture. Carefully turn the aubergine in the mix until coated. Spread into a single layer.

4   Put the dish into the hot oven and cook for about 10 minutes.

5   Remove the dish from the oven, close the lid and turn the timer to 15 minutes. Turn the aubergine pieces over, scatter over the pine nuts and put back into the hot oven.

6   Cook for 5–10 minutes until lightly browned, piping hot and cooked through. Season if necessary before serving with lemon wedges to squeeze over.

STUFFED AUBERGINES WITH MINT

This recipe is also delicious when made with sweet potatoes. You will need foil and a baking tray which fits in your oven.

SERVES 2		
	2 aubergines	10 mint leaves
	1 tbsp olive oil	Small bunch of fresh parsley
	2 tomatoes	Pinch of sugar
	2 garlic cloves	2 tsp liquid vegetable stock
	Small bunch of chives	Freshly milled salt and black pepper

1 Remove the lid from the halogen oven, place the low rack inside the oven and replace the lid. Preheat the oven to 200°C.

2 Trim and discard the aubergine stalks and rub with oil. Wrap in foil and put into the hot oven. Cook for 25–35 minutes until the aubergines are cooked, but not until they have collapsed.

3 Meanwhile, prepare the filling: finely chop the tomatoes, garlic, chives, mint leaves and parsley. Put them all into a bowl and stir in the sugar, liquid stock and seasoning.

4 Carefully cut the cooked aubergines in half and scoop out the pulp, leaving the outer shells intact. Finely chop or crush the aubergine pulp and stir into the tomato mixture. Spoon the filling into the aubergine cases. Lift them onto the tray and drizzle with oil. Put the tray into the hot oven and cook for 12–15 minutes until they are browned, piping hot and cooked through.

Red Pepper and Tomato Stew with Basil and Olives

There is an Italian feel to this simple stew, with a sunshine burst of ingredients. You will need an ovenproof dish which fits in your oven.

SERVES 4	2 red peppers	2 tbsp olive oil
	Large handful of basil leaves	400 g can chopped tomatoes
	2 garlic cloves	Pinch sugar
	10 stoned black olives	Freshly milled salt and black pepper

1   Remove the lid from the halogen oven, place the low rack inside the oven and replace the lid. Preheat the halogen oven to 200°C.

2   Cut the red peppers in half, remove and discard the seeds and stalks, and cut into thin slices. Tear the basil leaves into pieces, chop the garlic and halve the olives.

3   Pour the oil into the dish and stir in the pepper pieces. Put the dish into the hot oven and cook for 10–12 minutes until the peppers begin to sizzle.

4   Remove the dish from the oven, close the lid and turn the timer to 40 minutes. Pour the tomatoes over the red peppers and stir in the chopped garlic, half of the torn basil, the olive halves, sugar and seasoning.

5   Cover and put the dish into the hot oven and cook for 25 minutes until piping hot and cooked through. Stir in the remaining torn basil just before serving.

LEMON MINTED PEAS WITH CHINESE LEAVES AND SESAME SEEDS

Such a simple recipe to make – I'm sure we all have a bag of frozen peas lurking at the back of the freezer. Serve topped with a spoonful of thick yogurt. You will need a large, buttered, shallow ovenproof dish which fits in your oven.

SERVES 2–3	Large handful of Chinese leaves	500g/1 lb 2 oz minted peas, thawed if frozen
	6 spring onions	Freshly milled salt and black pepper
	1 small lemon	1 tbsp sesame seeds
	150 ml/¼ pint chicken or vegetable stock	

1   Remove the lid from the halogen oven, place the low rack inside the oven and replace the lid. Preheat the halogen oven to 200°C.

2   Thinly slice the Chinese leaves and the spring onions. Finely grate the rind from the lemon, cut in half and squeeze the juice. Stir the lemon rind and juice into the stock.

3   Tip the Chinese leaves, spring onions and peas into the buttered dish.

4   Season a little, pour over the flavoured stock and scatter over the sesame seeds.

5   Cover the dish and put into the hot oven. Cook for 25–35 minutes until piping hot and cooked through.

6   Cover the dish loosely with foil. Put the dish into the hot oven and cook for 20–25 minutes until piping hot and cooked through.

Oven Frittata

This is delicious served as a light meal on its own or cut into small wedges and served with drinks. You will need a buttered base-lined ovenproof dish about 20cm/8 inches in diameter which fits in your oven.

SERVES 2		
	1 cooked potato, about 150g/5½ oz	4 large eggs
	2 spring onions	Freshly milled salt and black pepper
	Small handful of mint leaves	2 tbsp olive oil
	Small handful of parsley leaves	1 tbsp butter
	50g/1¾ oz Red Leicester cheese	

1   Remove the lid from the halogen oven, place the high rack inside the oven and replace the lid. Preheat the oven to 180°C.

2   Cut the potato into small dice and thinly slice the spring onions. Finely chop the mint and parsley leaves and grate the cheese.

3   Break the eggs into a jug and beat with a little seasoning and the chopped mint and parsley.

4   Put the olive oil and butter into the dish and stir in the spring onions and diced potato.

5   Put the dish into the hot oven and cook for 6–8 minutes until the potato begins to soften and brown. Remove the dish from the oven, replace the lid and set the timer to 18 minutes.

6   Pour the egg mixture into the hot dish, tilting the dish to spread the mixture evenly. Sprinkle the cheese evenly over the top.

7   Put the dish back into the hot oven. Cook for 4–6 minutes until the egg is set, piping hot and cooked through. It will cook quickly, so keep an eye on it throughout.

Corn-on-the-Cob with Herb Butter

Choose cobs which are heavy for their size. You will need 4 large squares of foil.

SERVES 4	4 cobs of sweet corn 100g/3½ oz salted or unsalted butter 2 tbsp chopped chives 1 tbsp chopped parsley

1   Remove any leaves and silky strands from the corn cobs and soak them in a bowl of cold water for 45 minutes. Put the butter in a small bowl and stir until soft and creamy. Stir in the chopped chives and parsley.

2   Remove the lid from the halogen oven, place the low rack inside the oven and replace the lid. Preheat the halogen oven to 200°C.

3   Drain the corn cobs. Place each one on a foil square and top with some of the herb butter. Gather up the foil and seal securely.

4   Put the parcels directly on the rack in the hot oven and cook for 20–30 minutes until tender, depending on their size.

5   Give each person a parcel and let them spoon the melted butter over the cobs.

Sticky Roasted Carrots and Beetroot

Fabulous colours, as the orange carrots take on some of the deep red from the beetroot. You will need a large, shallow ovenproof dish which fits in your oven.

SERVES 4–6	
4 small beetroot	1 tbsp orange juice
5 carrots	2 tbsp vegetable oil
3 tbsp clear honey	Freshly milled salt and black pepper
1 tbsp red wine vinegar	

1   Remove the lid from the halogen oven, place the low rack inside the oven and replace the lid. Preheat the halogen oven to 200°C.

2   Trim the ends of the beetroot but do not peel. Cut into wedges. Cut the carrots into thick baton shapes.

3   Put the honey, vinegar, orange juice and oil into the dish. Put into the oven for 1–2 minutes to warm and melt the honey.

4   Remove the dish from the oven, close the lid and turn the timer to 30 minutes.

5   Put the beetroot and carrot pieces into the hot dish. Carefully turn in the honey mixture until coated and spread them to a single layer. Put the dish into the hot oven and cook for 15–25 minutes, turning once until the beetroot and carrot are golden, piping hot and cooked through. Season to taste before serving.

Green Bean and Green Pepper Thai Curry

The light and fragrant Thai flavours complement the beans and pak choi. You will need a wide ovenproof dish which fits in your oven.

SERVES 2		
	150g/5½ oz French beans	150ml/¼ pint chicken or vegetable bouillon powder
	100g/3½ oz sugar snap peas	150ml/¼ pint coconut milk
	1 green pepper	1 tbsp green Thai curry paste
	Large handful pak choi leaves, or Chinese leaves	1 tsp ginger paste
	Small bunch of fresh coriander	Freshly milled black pepper

1 Remove the lid from the halogen oven, place the low rack inside the oven and replace the lid. Preheat the oven to 200°C.

2 Put the kettle on to boil. Trim the French beans and sugar snap peas. Cut the green pepper in half, remove and discard the seeds and stalk, and cut into bite-sized pieces. Thinly slice the pak choi leaves, or Chinese leaves, and roughly chop the coriander.

3 Pour 150ml/¼ pint boiling water (from the kettle) into a jug and stir in the bouillon powder. Mix in the coconut milk, Thai curry paste, ginger paste and a little black pepper.

4 Put the French beans, sugar snap peas, green pepper, pak choi or Chinese leaves and coriander into the dish and pour over the stock mixture.

5 Put the dish into the hot oven and cook for 20–35 minutes or until the vegetables are tender, piping hot and cooked through.

2.

RICE, PASTA, GRAINS
AND BEANS

To CAPTURE AND ENHANCE FLAVOUR, and to give texture and interest to a dish, beans,
rice, pasta and grains are simply ideal. So too are chickpeas, polenta and couscous,
lentils and noodles, all of which are used in recipes in this chapter.

Of course, they achieve their effects in all sorts of ways. A fragrant or spiced rice mixture
is great with meat dishes, like turkey pilaf, whereas brown rice is nutty and chewy. Pasta and
noodles absorb and wrap around flavours in different ways, depending on their shape (see
Lasagne with Smoked Trout, page 62, and Salmon and Macaroni Bake, page 66). And beans,
in their great variety, offer us such tempting dishes as Lamb with Flageolet Beans (page 70)
and Hot and Sour Cannellini Beans and Sweetcorn (page 58).

So why not be like me and keep a plentiful supply of these versatile ingredients in your
store cupboard, always at the ready for a well-planned or impromptu meal from your
halogen oven?

CURRIED LENTILS

There are so many types of lentils to choose from. Split red lentils collapse and are great for this dhal-type dish. Serve with yogurt and chutneys and scoop up with hot nan bread or flat breads. You will need a deep ovenproof dish which fits in your oven.

SERVES 4		
	1 red onion	1 tbsp vegetable bouillon powder
	1 garlic clove	2 tsp lemon juice
	1 green chilli (see page 19)	½ tsp ground cumin
	2 tomatoes	1 tsp ground coriander
	1 tbsp sunflower oil	Freshly milled black pepper
	200g/7 oz split red lentils	

1   Remove the lid from the halogen oven, place the low rack inside the oven and replace the lid. Preheat the halogen oven to 200°C.

2   Put the kettle on to boil. Finely chop the onion and garlic. Cut the chilli in half, remove and discard the seeds and stalks, and finely chop. Roughly chop the tomatoes.

3   Pour the oil into the dish and stir in the onion. Put into the hot oven and cook for 3–5 minutes until the onion begins to soften and brown.

4   Remove the lid from the oven and lift out the dish. Replace the lid, and set the timer for 60 minutes. Tip the lentils onto the softened onion and stir in the tomatoes, garlic, chilli, vegetable bouillon powder, lemon juice, cumin, coriander, a little black pepper and 700ml/1¼ pints boiling water (from the kettle).

5   Cover, return to the oven and continue cooking for 50 minutes – 1¼ hours in total, stirring once or twice, until piping hot and cooked through. Season if necessary.

Couscous with Prawns and Spinach

Couscous is made from semolina or cracked wheat, and picks up all the delicious flavours of this dish. You will need a large ovenproof dish which fits in your oven.

SERVES 2		
	1 small onion	1 tbsp olive oil
	3 tomatoes	1 tbsp liquid vegetable stock
	1 lemon	1 tbsp pine nuts
	Handful of spinach leaves	200g/7 oz cooked, shelled prawns
	200g/7 oz couscous	Freshly milled salt and black pepper

1   Remove the lid from the halogen oven, place the low rack inside the oven and replace the lid. Preheat the halogen oven to 200°C.

2   Put the kettle on to boil. Finely chop the onion. Roughly chop the tomatoes. Finely grate the rind from the lemon, cut in half and squeeze out the juice. If large, roughly chop the spinach leaves.

3   Put the couscous into a large bowl and pour over boiling water (from the kettle) to cover. Leave to stand, stirring occasionally.

4   Pour the oil into the dish and stir in the onion. Put into the hot oven and cook for 3–5 minutes until the onion begins to soften and brown.

5   Drain the couscous.

6   Remove the dish from the oven and set the timer to 35 minutes. Stir into the softened onion the tomatoes, lemon rind and juice, spinach, liquid stock, pine nuts, prawns, a little seasoning and 150ml/¼ pint boiling water (from the kettle). Stir in the drained couscous, cover and cook for 20–25 minutes until piping hot and cooked through. Serve immediately.

Falafels with Coriander Dressing in Hot Pitta Breads

Spices and chickpeas are the basis of these small 'burgers'. For a change, replace the pitta bread with flatbreads, soft tortillas or pancakes. You will need an oiled baking tray which fits in your oven.

SERVES 2	2 garlic cloves	Freshly milled salt and black pepper
	Small bunch of fresh coriander	Sunflower oil
	200g can chickpeas	2 pitta breads
	1 tbsp tahini, sesame seed paste	2 spring onions
	2 tsp lemon juice	2 tomatoes
	1 tsp ground cardamom	300ml/½ pint natural yogurt
	1 tsp ground coriander	Selection of salad leaves

1   Remove the lid from the halogen oven, place the low rack inside the oven and replace the lid – later you will also use the high rack. Preheat the halogen oven to 200°C.

2   Crush the garlic. Finely chop the coriander.

3   Drain the chickpeas into a bowl and stir in half of the chopped coriander, the garlic, tahini, lemon juice, cardamom, ground coriander and a little pepper. With a fork crush the chickpeas and mix together well – I often use a potato masher.

4   With wetted hands, divide and shape the mixture into six balls and slightly flatten each one. Put the falafels on the oiled tray, leaving a space between each one.

5   Wrap the pitta breads in foil and put on the low rack in the hot oven. Put the high rack and tray of falafels into the oven and cook for 3–5 minutes on each side until browned and cooked through.

6   Thinly slice the spring onions and tomatoes. Pour the yogurt into a bowl and stir in the remaining chopped coriander and a little seasoning to taste.

7   Cut open the warm pitta breads and fill with the salad leaves, sliced spring onions and tomatoes, falafels and some of the yogurt dressing.

POLENTA WITH ROASTED RED PEPPER, OLIVES AND MOZZARELLA

Polenta, made from cornmeal, is available in ready-made blocks to be cut into slices, bars or cubes. Here I've used slices as the perfect shape to hold the spicy topping. Serve with salad leaves and hot bread. You will need a large baking tray which fits in your oven.

SERVES 4 as a snack, or 2 as a quick meal	200g/7 oz roasted red pepper 6 stoned black olives 1 tbsp pesto 1 tbsp pine nuts	Piece of mozzarella cheese, about 100g/3½ oz 500g block of ready-made polenta 1 tbsp olive oil Large handful of rocket leaves

1   Remove the lid from the halogen oven, place the high rack inside the oven and replace the lid. Preheat the halogen oven to 200°C.

2   Cut the roasted pepper into thin strips and slice the olives. Put the pepper and olives into a bowl and stir in the pesto and pine nuts.

3   Tear the mozzarella cheese into shreds.

4   Slice the block of polenta horizontally into four.

5   Brush both sides of the polenta slices with a little of the oil and arrange on the tray.

6   Put the tray into the hot oven and cook for 6–9 minutes until browned. Turn the polenta slices over and cook a further 6–9 minutes until browned and heated through. Spoon some of the red pepper mixture on each slice and top with pieces of the mozzarella cheese. Cook for 3–5 minutes or until the cheese has melted and the polenta is piping hot and cooked through. Serve immediately, topped with rocket leaves which will begin to wilt from the heat.

BROWN RICE WITH PANCETTA AND COURGETTE

Pancetta is Italian, cured, unsmoked bacon; just a small amount gives lots of flavour to a dish. Brown rice is slightly chewy and has a nut-like flavour, but you could use basmati or red Camargue rice instead. You will need a wide ovenproof dish which fits in your oven.

SERVES 2	125g/4½ oz long grain brown rice	60g/2¼ oz pancetta
	1 small red onion	2 tsp olive oil
	1 garlic clove	2 tsp vegetable bouillon powder
	2 sage leaves	Freshly milled salt and black pepper
	1 small bunch fresh parsley	3 tbsp grated cheese
	1 courgette	

1 Remove the lid from the halogen oven, place the low rack inside the oven and replace the lid. Preheat the halogen oven to 200°C.

2 Put the kettle on to boil. Cook the rice according to the packet instructions and drain. Finely chop the onion and crush the garlic. Tear the sage leaves in half and finely chop the parsley. Finely chop the courgette and the pancetta.

3 Pour the oil into the dish and stir in the onion, garlic, courgette, pancetta and sage leaves.

4 Put the dish into the hot oven and cook for 3–5 minutes until the ingredients begin to soften.

5 Pour 150ml/¼ pint boiling water (from the kettle) into a jug and stir in the bouillon powder and a little seasoning.

6 Remove the dish from the oven and set the timer to 30 minutes. Pour the stock into the dish and stir in the parsley, cooked rice and cheese. Loosely cover and cook for 25–35 minutes or until piping hot and cooked through. Serve immediately.

HOT AND SOUR CANNELLINI BEANS AND SWEETCORN

A very simple dish using store-cupboard ingredients. A meal in itself, it could also be an accompaniment to roasted meats or fish. You will need an ovenproof dish which fits in your oven.

SERVES 2–3		
	410g can cannellini beans	1 tbsp tamarind paste
	198g can sweetcorn	1 tbsp light soy sauce
	6 cherry tomatoes	1 tbsp lemon juice
	2 vegetable stock cubes	Freshly milled salt and black pepper

1 Remove the lid from the halogen oven, place the low rack inside the oven and replace the lid. Preheat the halogen oven to 200°C.

2 Put the kettle on to boil. Drain the cans of beans and sweetcorn and tip into the dish. Halve the cherry tomatoes and put into the dish.

3 Pour 400ml/14 fl oz boiling water (from the kettle) into a jug and stir in the stock cubes, tamarind paste, soy sauce, lemon juice and a little seasoning.

4 Stir the stock mixture into the beans and tomatoes, cover and put into the hot oven.

5 Cook for 50–60 minutes or until piping hot and cooked through.

SPICED BEANS WITH SQUASH

If squash is not in season, use pumpkin or marrow. You will need a wide ovenproof dish which fits in your oven.

SERVES 2–3		
	1 onion	1 tbsp vegetable bouillon powder
	1 garlic clove	1 tsp cumin seeds
	350g/12 oz piece of squash	1 tsp ground cardamom
	400g can black-eyed beans	½ tsp ground smoked paprika pepper
	2 tbsp oil	Freshly milled black pepper

1 Remove the lid from the halogen oven, place the low rack inside the oven and replace the lid. Preheat the halogen oven to 190°C.

2 Finely chop the onion and crush the garlic. Peel the squash, scoop out and discard any seeds and cut into small cubes. Drain the beans. Put the kettle on to boil.

3 Arrange the onion, garlic and squash in the dish and drizzle with the oil.

4 Put the dish into the hot oven and cook for 4–6 minutes until the onion softens and the pieces of squash are beginning to brown.

5 Pour 425ml/¾ pint boiling water (from the kettle) into a jug and stir in the bouillon powder, cumin seeds, cardamom, paprika and a little black pepper.

6 Remove the lid from the oven and lift out the dish. Replace the lid, and set the timer for 60 minutes. Tip the beans into the hot dish and stir in the stock mixture.

7 Cover and put the dish into the hot oven. Cook for 1¼–1½ hours until piping hot and cooked through. Look at the dish after 55 minutes; it may be ready.

Turkey Pilaf

It needs only a green salad to make a complete meal. You will need a wide ovenproof dish which fits in your oven.

SERVES 2–3		
	250g/9 oz skinless boneless turkey	½ tsp ground cinnamon
	1 red onion	Freshly milled salt and black pepper
	140g/5 oz basmati rice	Small handful of sultanas
	1 tbsp sunflower oil	1 tbsp chopped parsley
	1 tbsp chicken bouillon powder	A few toasted flaked almonds, optional
	2–3 tsp curry paste	

1   Remove the lid from the halogen oven, place the low rack inside the oven and replace the lid. Preheat the halogen oven to 200°C.

2   Put the kettle on to boil. Cut the turkey into small bite-sized pieces and very thinly slice the onion.

3   Cook the rice according to the packet instructions and drain.

4   Arrange the onion and turkey pieces in the dish and drizzle with the oil. Put the dish into the hot oven and cook for 4–6 minutes until the onion and turkey begin to brown.

5   Pour 300ml/½ pint boiling water (from the kettle) into a jug and stir in the bouillon powder, curry paste, cinnamon and a little seasoning.

6   Remove the lid from the oven and lift out the dish. Replace the lid, and set the timer for 40 minutes. Pour the stock mixture into the hot dish and stir in the cooked rice and sultanas, then cover.

7   Put the dish into the hot oven and cook for 30–40 minutes until piping hot and the turkey is cooked through. Fluff the mixture with a fork and mix in the chopped parsley. Scatter over the almonds, if using, and serve immediately.

LASAGNE WITH SMOKED TROUT

A simplified fishy version of a traditional lasagne. Serve on its own with garlic bread and crisp salad leaves. You will need a wide shallow ovenproof dish which fits in your oven.

SERVES 2–3

1 lemon
2 smoked trout fillets
55g/2 oz mature Cheddar cheese
115g/4 oz ricotta cheese
4 tbsp milk
¼ tsp ground nutmeg
2 tbsp wholegrain mustard
Freshly milled salt and black pepper

227g can crushed tomatoes
1 tsp harissa sauce
1 tbsp chopped parsley
3 large fresh pasta lasagne sheets, about 14cm/5½ inches x 20cm/8 inches
2 tbsp grated Parmesan cheese

1. Remove the lid from the halogen oven, place the low rack inside the oven and replace the lid. Preheat the halogen oven to 200°C.

2. Grate the lemon, cut in half and squeeze out the juice. Flake the trout, removing the skin and bones. Grate the Cheddar cheese. Spoon the ricotta cheese into a bowl and mix in the milk, nutmeg, mustard, half of the grated Cheddar cheese and seasoning. Add a little more milk if very thick.

3. Tip the tomatoes into a bowl and stir in the harissa sauce, parsley and a little seasoning.

4. Spoon a third of the tomato mixture into the dish and cover with a sheet of lasagne. Spread with another third of the tomato mix, and cover with half of the flaked trout. Pour over one third of the cheese mixture then cover with a sheet of lasagne. Cover with the remaining tomato mixture and flaked trout. Pour over half of the cheese mixture. Top with the last sheet of lasagne and the rest of the Cheddar cheese mixture.

5. Sprinkle over the remaining grated cheese and Parmesan and loosely cover with foil. Put the dish into the hot oven and cook for 1¼–1½ hours, but look at it after 55 minutes in case it is ready. Cook until lightly browned, piping hot and cooked through.

Chicken Sweet and Sour Savoury Rice

A bright and colourful dish, a great way to use up those leftovers. You will need a greased ovenproof dish which fits in your oven.

SERVES 2		
	1 small red pepper	Small handful sweetcorn
	2 spring onions	150ml/¼ pint chicken stock
	Small handful spinach leaves	4 tbsp hot sweet and sour sauce
	255g/8 oz boneless cooked chicken	250g/9 oz cooked long-grain or basmati rice
	Small handful peas	Freshly milled salt and black pepper

1 Remove the lid from the halogen oven, place the low rack inside the oven and replace the lid. Preheat the halogen oven to 200°C.

2 Cut the pepper in half, remove and discard the seeds and stalk, and finely chop. Thinly slice the spring onions. Finely shred the spinach leaves. Cut the chicken into very small bite-sized pieces.

3 Put the red pepper, spring onions, peas and sweetcorn into the dish and pour over the stock. Put into the hot oven and cook for 10–12 minutes until the vegetables have softened.

4 Remove the lid from the oven and lift out the dish. Replace the lid, and set the timer for 40 minutes.

5 Stir the sweet and sour sauce, spinach, chicken, rice and seasoning into the hot vegetables and cover. Put back into the hot oven and cook for 20–35 minutes or until piping hot and cooked through.

Chorizo and Rice with Mustard and Sesame Seeds

Chorizo is a highly spiced Spanish sausage – for something milder, use Frankfurter sausages. You will need a wide ovenproof dish which fits in your oven.

SERVES 2	125g/4½ oz long grain white rice	1 tbsp chicken or vegetable bouillon powder
	1 carrot	Freshly milled salt and black pepper
	Small bunch of fresh parsley	2 tsp mustard seeds
	200g/7 oz chorizo sausage	3 tsp sesame seeds
	2 tsp sunflower oil	

1 Remove the lid from the halogen oven, place the low rack inside the oven and replace the lid. Preheat the halogen oven to 200°C.

2 Put the kettle on to boil. Cook the rice according to the packet instructions and drain. Coarsely grate the carrot and finely chop the parsley. Thinly slice the chorizo sausage.

3 Pour the oil into the dish and stir in the chorizo sausage.

4 Put the dish into the hot oven and cook for 4–6 minutes until the chorizo begins to cook and brown.

5 Pour 400ml/14 fl oz boiling water into a jug and stir in the bouillon powder and seasoning.

6 Remove the dish from the oven and set the timer to 40 minutes. Pour the stock into the dish and stir in the grated carrot, parsley, cooked rice, mustard and sesame seeds. Loosely cover and cook for 25–35 minutes or until piping hot and cooked through – the carrot will have a slight crunch. Serve immediately.

SALMON AND MACARONI BAKE

Macaroni cheese with a twist. Use any type of short pasta tubes to make this tasty dish. You will need an ovenproof dish which fits in your oven.

SERVES 2–3	225g/8 oz skinless salmon pieces	Freshly milled salt and black pepper
	3 tomatoes	100g/3½ oz macaroni pasta
	Small handful of fresh fennel leaves	150ml/¼ pint low-fat crème fraîche
	1 lemon	2 tbsp milk
	2 tbsp fish or vegetable stock	50g/1¾ oz grated Cheddar cheese

1   Remove the lid from the halogen oven, place the low rack inside the oven and replace the lid. Preheat the halogen oven to 200°C.

2   Cut the salmon into bite-sized pieces, removing any bones. Thinly slice the tomatoes and chop the fennel leaves. Squeeze the juice from the lemon.

3   Arrange the tomato slices over the base of the dish and scatter over the salmon pieces. Sprinkle over the chopped fennel, pour over the lemon juice and stock and add a little seasoning. Cover with foil.

4   Put the dish into the hot oven and cook for 12–15 minutes until the salmon is almost cooked.

5   Cook the macaroni according to the packet instructions and drain.

6   Put the hot macaroni into a bowl and stir in the crème fraîche, milk and seasoning.

7   Remove the lid from the oven and lift out the dish. Replace the lid, and set the timer for 20 minutes.

8   Quickly spoon the creamy macaroni over the salmon and sprinkle over the grated Cheddar cheese. Put back into the hot oven and cook for 10–15 minutes until piping hot and cooked through.

COUSCOUS WITH CHICKEN AND APRICOTS

If you prefer a little 'heat' in the dish, add a tablespoon or two of sweet chilli sauce with the other seasonings. You will need a large oiled ovenproof dish which fits in your oven.

SERVES 3–4

1 red onion
2 garlic cloves
Handful of coriander leaves
1 lime
5 ready-to-eat dried apricots
3 boneless, skinless chicken breasts

300g/10½ oz couscous
Freshly milled salt and black pepper
2 tbsp liquid chicken stock
2 tbsp vegetable oil
2 tbsp tomato and chilli relish

1   Remove the lid from the halogen oven, place the low rack inside the oven and replace the lid. Preheat the halogen oven to 200°C.

2   Put the kettle on to boil. Finely chop the onion and garlic. Roughly chop the coriander leaves. Finely grate the rind from the lime, cut in half and squeeze the juice. Cut the dried apricots into thin strips. Thinly slice the chicken breasts.

3   Put the couscous into a large bowl and pour over boiling water (from the kettle) to cover. Stir in the liquid stock and a little seasoning. Leave to stand, stirring occasionally.

4   Pour the oil into the dish and stir in the onion, garlic and chicken pieces. Put into the hot oven and cook for 10–12 minutes until golden brown.

5   Drain the couscous.

6   Remove the lid from the oven and lift out the dish. Replace the lid, and set the timer for 35 minutes. Stir into the browned chicken, onion and garlic, strips of apricots, coriander leaves, the lime rind and juice, liquid stock, relish, a little seasoning and 250ml/9 fl oz boiling water (from the kettle). Stir in the drained couscous.

7   Cover the dish loosely with foil. Put the dish into the hot oven and cook for 20–25 minutes until piping hot and cooked through. Serve immediately.

BACON AND PASTA CHEESE

This is a useful weekday dish, simple but very tasty and comforting. You will need an ovenproof dish which fits in your oven.

SERVES 2–3	
4 rashers smoked back bacon	2 tbsp chicken or vegetable stock
1 small onion	2 tbsp milk
Large handful of parsley leaves	50g/1¾ oz grated mature Red Leicester cheese
2 tsp vegetable oil	Freshly milled salt and black pepper
100g/3½ oz fresh pasta bows or spirals	2–3 tbsp grated Parmesan cheese
300ml/½ pint prepared white sauce	

1   Remove the lid from the halogen oven, place the low rack inside the oven and replace the lid. Preheat the halogen oven to 180°C.

2   Put the kettle on to boil. With scissors snip any rinds from the bacon rashers and cut into bite-sized pieces. Finely chop the onion and tear the parsley leaves into small pieces.

3   Pour the oil into the dish and stir in the onion and bacon pieces. Put into the hot oven and cook for 4–5 minutes until golden brown.

4   Cook the pasta according to the packet instructions and drain.

5   Remove the lid from the oven and lift out the dish. Replace the lid, and set the timer for 25 minutes. Stir into the hot dish the white sauce, stock, milk, grated Red Leicester cheese, parsley and a little seasoning. Stir in the drained pasta and sprinkle over the Parmesan cheese.

6   Put the dish back into the hot oven and cook for 10–15 minutes until piping hot and cooked through. Serve immediately.

LAMB WITH FLAGEOLET BEANS

I have made this dish with lamb, but it works equally well with chicken or beef. You will need a large ovenproof dish which fits in your oven.

SERVES 4	450g/1 lb lean boneless lamb	1 tbsp lamb or vegetable bouillon powder
	2 shallots	1 tbsp tomato purée
	Small bunch of fresh tarragon	150ml/¼ pint passata, sieved tomatoes
	400g can flageolet beans	Freshly milled salt and black pepper
	2 tbsp olive oil	2 bay leaves

1   Remove the lid from the halogen oven, place the low rack inside the oven and replace the lid. Preheat the halogen oven to 200°C.

2   Trim any excess fat from the lamb and cut into small bite-sized pieces. Finely chop the shallots. Pull the leaves off the tarragon stalks and finely chop. Drain the flageolet beans.

3   Arrange the lamb and chopped shallots in the dish and drizzle over the oil. Put the dish into the hot oven and cook for 6–8 minutes until beginning to brown.

4   Put the kettle on to boil. Put the bouillon powder into a jug and pour over 300ml/½ pint boiling water (from the kettle) and stir in the tomato purée, passata and a little seasoning.

5   Remove the dish from the oven and set the timer to 60 minutes. Pour the hot stock mix over the browned shallots and lamb and stir in the flageolet beans, bay leaves and chopped tarragon.

6   Cover the dish and cook for 1¼–1½ hours until the lamb is tender, piping hot and cooked through.

BREAKFAST RICE WITH SAUSAGE AND MUSHROOMS

A delicious filling dish for breakfast or brunch. Serve with brown sauce or tomato ketchup. You will need a large shallow ovenproof dish which fits in your oven.

SERVES 2–3

125g/4½ oz long grain white rice
1 small red onion
5 pork sausages
8 button mushrooms

2 tsp vegetable oil
1 tbsp French mustard
Freshly milled salt and black pepper

1. Remove the lid from the halogen oven, place the low rack inside the oven and replace the lid. Preheat the halogen oven to 200°C.

2. Put the kettle on to boil. With the boiling water, cook the rice according to the packet instructions and drain.

3. Finely chop the onion and cut each sausage into three or four. Quarter the mushrooms.

4. Pour the oil into the dish and stir in the sausages and mushrooms.

5. Put the dish into the hot oven and cook for 4-6 minutes until the sausages and mushrooms begin to cook and brown.

6. Remove the lid from the oven and lift out the dish. Replace the lid, and set the timer for 30 minutes. Stir the cooked rice, mustard and a little seasoning into the sausages and mushrooms and cover. Put back into the hot oven and cook for 20–30 minutes until piping hot and cooked through.

Noodles with Seafood and Fennel

Make this into 'surf and turf' by adding some sliced frankfurter sausages or bite-sized pieces of cooked chicken or turkey, and serve with green salad and garlic bread. You will need a wide ovenproof dish which fits in your oven.

SERVES 2		
½ lemon		150g/5½ oz noodles
Large bunch of fennel		2 tbsp sunflower oil
Small bunch of chives		150ml/¼ pint soured cream
250g/9 oz mixed seafood, such as shelled prawns,		2 tbsp fish or vegetable stock
skinless trout or salmon fillets		Freshly milled salt and black pepper

1   Remove the lid from the halogen oven, place the low rack inside the oven and replace the lid. Preheat the halogen oven to 200°C.

2   Finely grate the rind from the lemon, and squeeze the juice. Chop the fennel and slice the chives. Cut the seafood into bite-sized pieces.

3   Put the kettle on to boil. With the boiling water, cook the noodles according to the packet instructions and drain.

4   Pour the oil into the dish and stir in the seafood pieces. Put into the hot oven and cook for 6–8 minutes until just beginning to change colour.

5   Remove the lid from the oven and lift out the dish. Replace the lid, and set the timer for 25 minutes. Carefully stir into the seafood mixture, the lemon rind and juice, fennel, chives, soured cream, stock and seasoning. Fold in the drained noodles.

6   Cover the dish loosely with foil. Put the dish into the hot oven and cook for 12–15 minutes until piping hot and cooked through. Serve immediately.

LENTILS WITH BACON AND SAUSAGES

A rustic dish, and very satisfying. Serve with pickles, crusty bread and a watercress salad. You will need a wide ovenproof dish which fits in your oven.

SERVES 2–3

1 small onion
3 rashers back bacon
4 large farmhouse sausages, herb or spicy
2 tsp olive oil
1 tbsp vegetable bouillon powder
1 tbsp brown sauce

1 tbsp tomato purée
Freshly milled salt and black pepper
175g/6 oz ready-to-eat puy lentils, or, 85g/3 oz lentils cooked according to the packet instructions and drained

1   Remove the lid from the halogen oven, place the low rack inside the oven and replace the lid. Preheat the halogen oven to 200°C.

2   Put the kettle on to boil. Thinly slice the onion. With scissors, trim the rind from the bacon and cut into strips. Slice each sausage into four.

3   Arrange the onion, bacon strips and sausage pieces in the dish and drizzle with the oil.

4   Put the dish into the hot oven and cook for 4–6 minutes until the onion softens and the bacon and sausages are beginning to brown.

5   Pour 300ml/½ pint boiling water (from the kettle) into a jug and stir in the bouillon powder, brown sauce, tomato purée and a little seasoning.

6   Remove the lid from the oven and lift out the dish. Replace the lid, and set the timer for 25 minutes. Tip the lentils into the hot dish and stir in the stock mixture.

7   Put the dish into the hot oven and cook for 15–20 minutes until piping hot and cooked through. Cover if it browns too much.

PINTO BEANS WITH RATATOUILLE

This tastes great hot or cold. Replace the pinto beans with chickpeas or flageolet beans. You will need a large wide ovenproof dish which fits in your oven.

SERVES 4		
	1 red onion	2 tbsp olive oil
	2 garlic cloves	300ml/½ pint vegetable or chicken stock
	2 red peppers	400g can tomatoes
	4 courgettes	Pinch sugar
	Large bunch of basil leaves	Freshly milled salt and black pepper
	410g can pinto beans	

1. Remove the lid from the halogen oven, place the low rack inside the oven and replace the lid. Preheat the halogen oven to 180°C.

2. Finely chop the onion and garlic. Cut the red peppers in half, remove and discard the seeds and stalks, and cut into thin slices. Trim the courgettes and cut into small dice. Tear the basil leaves into pieces. Drain and rinse the pinto beans.

3. Pour the oil into the dish and stir in the onion and garlic, peppers and courgettes. Put into the hot oven and cook for 15–20 minutes until just beginning to soften and brown a little.

4. Remove the lid from the oven and lift out the dish. Replace the lid, and set the timer for 55 minutes. Stir in the pinto beans, stock, tomatoes, sugar, seasoning and half the basil.

5. Cover and put the dish into the hot oven. Cook for 45–55 minutes and check if the vegetables are soft; if not cook a further 15–20 minutes or until piping hot and cooked through. If necessary add a little more stock. Stir in the remaining chopped basil leaves before serving.

Linguine with Clams and Courgettes

I've used linguine, but pick your favourite pasta or noodles. Serve with crusty bread to mop up the juices. You will need a large shallow ovenproof dish which fits in your oven.

SERVES 2–3	
350g/12 oz clams in their shells	150ml/¼ pint fish stock
1 lemon	¼ tsp chilli paste
5 baby courgettes	Freshly milled salt and black pepper
Small bunch of dill	350g/12 oz fresh linguine pasta
2 tbsp olive oil	2 tsp fish or chicken bouillon powder
150ml/¼ pint dry white wine	

1 Remove the lid from the halogen oven, place the high rack inside the oven and replace the lid. Preheat the halogen oven to 200°C.

2 Clean the clams in cold water and discard any which are open. Finely grate the rind from half of the lemon, cut in half and squeeze the juice from both halves. Trim the courgettes and thinly slice. Chop the dill.

3 Pour the oil into the dish and stir in the sliced courgettes. Put into the hot oven and cook for 6–8 minutes until just beginning to soften and change colour.

4 Remove the lid from the oven and lift out the dish. Replace the lid, and set the timer for 25 minutes. Pour the wine and fish stock over the courgettes and stir in the lemon rind and juice, chilli paste, dill and a little seasoning. Put the dish back into the hot oven and cook for 6–8 minutes until hot and bubbling.

5 Remove the lid from the oven and stir the clams into the hot dish. Replace the lid and cook for 6–8 minutes, stirring once or twice until the clams have opened. Discard any unopened shells.

6 Meanwhile, put the kettle on to boil. With the boiling water and the bouillon powder, cook the linguine according to the packet instructions and drain.

7 Spoon the clam and courgette mixture over the hot linguine and serve immediately.

CREAMY NOODLES WITH MIXED MUSHROOMS AND SPINACH

The noodles are cooked before being added to the halogen oven. Choose your favourite type of noodle from the huge number available. You will need a wide ovenproof dish which fits in your oven.

SERVES 2		
	Small bunch of chives	1 tsp lemon juice
	1 sprig of fresh thyme	150ml/¼ pint crème fraîche
	200g/7 oz mixed mushrooms, such as shiitake, chestnut, button or oyster	3 tbsp dry white vermouth
	150g/5½ oz noodles	Freshly milled salt and black pepper
	2 tbsp sunflower oil	Small handful of small spinach leaves
		1 tbsp grated Parmesan cheese

1   Remove the lid from the halogen oven, place the low rack inside the oven and replace the lid. Preheat the halogen oven to 200°C.

2   Thinly slice the chives and pull the leaves from the sprig of thyme. Trim the mushrooms and cut them into small bite-sized pieces.

3   Cook the noodles according to the packet instructions and drain.

4   Pour the oil into the dish and stir in the mushrooms. Put the dish into the hot oven and cook for 2–4 minutes until they begin to soften.

5   Remove the dish from the oven and set the timer to 20 minutes. Stir into the softened mushrooms, the lemon juice, crème fraîche, vermouth, chives, thyme and seasoning. Fold in the drained noodles and spinach leaves. Sprinkle over the cheese. Loosely cover and cook for 12–15 minutes until piping hot and cooked through. Serve immediately.

3. Meat, Poultry and Game

TENDER LAMB OR PORK, flavoursome beef or a succulent chicken, together with accompanying vegetables – these are likely to be among the first meals you will be eager to prepare when you acquire your halogen oven. And when you see what success this brings, they are sure to become a mainstay of your repertoire.

For regular family meals and for special occasions, meat dishes are always going to be firm favourites, with their rich and subtle flavours enhanced by the well-judged use of exciting spices and aromatic herbs. Just look through the enticing recipes in this chapter to discover Roast Lamb with Spiced Fennel and Courgette Stuffing (page 90), Pheasant Casserole with Orange, Coriander and Sliced Potato Topping (page 108), Turkey Joint with Parma Ham, Parmesan and Fresh Herbs (page 82), and a good deal more.

Many of these recipes would be suitable for freezing, so if you find some left over you can save it for another day.

CHICKEN CURRY

Choose whatever flavour of curry paste you like. Serve with poppadoms, chutneys and basmati rice. You will need a large shallow ovenproof dish which fits in your oven.

SERVES 4	4 chicken joints	300ml/½ pint natural yogurt
	2 garlic cloves	2 tbsp tomato purée
	Small piece of root ginger	Sunflower oil
	½ lime	Freshly milled salt and black pepper
	1 tbsp curry paste	2 red onions
	1 tbsp chilli sauce	2 tbsp ground almonds

1   Cut three to four gashes across the top of the chicken joints and dry with kitchen paper. Crush the garlic cloves, grate the ginger and squeeze the juice from the lime.

2   Put the garlic, ginger and lime juice into a large non-metallic bowl and mix in the curry paste, chilli sauce, yogurt, tomato purée, 1 tbsp of the oil, 2 tbsp cold water and a little seasoning.

3   Put the chicken joints into the bowl and turn in the spice mixture until thoroughly coated. Cover with clear film and chill for 3–4 hours to allow the marinade to get into the chicken.

4   Remove the lid from the halogen oven, place the low and high racks inside the oven and replace the lid. Preheat the halogen oven to 200°C.

5   Thinly slice the onions and put onto a piece of foil, drizzle over a little oil and put into the hot oven. Cook for 15–20 minutes whilst you prepare the rest of the recipe.

6   Lift the chicken from the marinade and arrange in the dish. Stir the ground almonds into the remaining marinade and spoon over the chicken. Drizzle over a little oil.

7   Remove the lid from the oven and put the onions on the foil on the low rack; if browned, fold the foil to make a parcel. Replace the high rack and put the dish of chicken into the hot oven. Replace the lid and cook for 10–15 minutes, turning once, until lightly browned on both sides. Cover and cook for a further 15–20 minutes until the chicken is piping hot and cooked through. Serve with the roasted onions scattered on top.

Turkey Joint with Parma Ham, Parmesan and Fresh Herbs

The flavours of Italy, or more especially of Parma, famed for its ham and for Parmesan cheese. The bacon and Parma ham complement the turkey and keep it moist, allowing the aromatic herbs to work their magic. You will need a shallow dish or roasting tin which fits in your oven.

SERVES 3–4

Small bunch of fresh parsley
Small bunch of fresh chervil
Small bunch of fresh chives
2 spring onions
2 tbsp freshly grated Parmesan cheese

Freshly milled salt and black pepper
700g/1 lb 9 oz boneless turkey breast joint, skinned
6 rashers streaky bacon
6 rashers Parma ham
2 tbsp olive oil

1 Remove the lid from the halogen oven, place the low rack inside the oven and replace the lid. Preheat the halogen oven to 190°C.

2 Finely chop the parsley, chervil and chives and thinly slice the spring onions. Put into a small bowl and stir in the grated cheese and a little seasoning.

3 Cut a wide pocket into the side of the turkey joint and stuff with the herb mixture. Press the joint back into shape.

4 With scissors, cut the rind from the bacon. Run the back of a knife along each rasher of bacon and Parma ham to flatten and stretch them.

5 Wrap alternating rashers of bacon and Parma ham around the turkey joint. Tie with string to keep the rashers in place. Put into the dish or roasting tin with the oil, cover with foil and cook in the hot oven for 20 minutes. Turn the turkey over, cover and cook for a further 20 minutes. Turn the turkey over, open the foil and cook for a further 10–15 minutes until browned, piping hot and cooked through. Serve sliced with the pan juices spooned over.

CHICKEN, BACON AND RED PEPPER WITH CHEESE TOASTS

Cheese on toast is a simple, effective alternative to the usual pastry topping on pies. You will need a deep ovenproof dish which fits in your oven.

SERVES 4		
	1 small onion	300ml/½ pint milk
	1 small red pepper	1 tsp dried mixed herbs
	350g/12 oz boneless chicken	Freshly milled salt and black pepper
	4 rashers back bacon	85g/3 oz butter
	2 tsp sunflower oil	6 French bread slices, or enough to cover the dish
	25g/1 oz plain flour	25g/1 oz finely grated cheese

1 Remove the lid from the halogen oven, place the low/high rack inside the oven and replace the lid. Preheat the halogen oven to 190°C.

2 Finely chop the onion. Cut the pepper in half, remove and discard the seeds and stalk, and finely chop. Cut the chicken into bite-sized pieces. With scissors, trim the rind from the bacon and cut into strips.

3 Put the onion, red pepper, chicken and bacon into the dish. Drizzle over the oil and put into the hot oven. Cook for 10–12 minutes until beginning to brown.

4 Put the flour, milk, herbs, a little seasoning and 25g/1 oz of the butter into a saucepan. Whisking continuously, bring to the boil and cook for 2 minutes.

5 Stir the hot sauce into the chicken mixture, cover and cook for a further 15 minutes.

6 Brush each slice of bread with a little of the remaining butter and sprinkle a little cheese on top. Arrange on top of the hot dish and cook for a further 10 minutes until piping hot and cooked through.

CRISP DUCK BREAST WITH POMEGRANATE SALAD

If time allows, leave the duck to marinate for a couple of hours or in the fridge overnight for the flavours to develop. You will need a shallow roasting tin which fits in your oven.

SERVES 2		Salad
	1 garlic clove	2 tbsp olive oil
	½ orange	1 tbsp red wine vinegar
	2 tbsp light soy sauce	Freshly milled salt and black pepper
	2 tsp five-spice powder	1 pomegranate
	2 tbsp marmalade or clear honey	Large bunch of watercress
	2 boneless duck breasts	Large handful of celery leaves

1   Remove the lid from the halogen oven, place the low rack inside the oven and replace the lid. Preheat the halogen oven to 220°C.

2   Crush the garlic and put into the roasting tin. Squeeze the juice from the orange into the dish and stir in the soy sauce, five-spice powder and marmalade or honey.

3   With a sharp knife, make several diagonal slashes in the fat of each duck breast (without cutting through into the meat). Put them into the dish and turn to coat in the mixture. Cover and chill – see opposite.

4   Put the duck breasts into the roasting tin, spooning over any extra marinade.

5   Put the roasting tin into the hot oven and cook for 15–20 minutes, turning once. Cook until browned, piping hot and cooked through.

6   Make the salad. Pour the oil and vinegar into a bowl and stir in a little seasoning. Cut the pomegranate in half and scoop the seeds into the dressing. Tear the watercress and celery leaves and add to the bowl. Stir to coat and serve immediately with the cooked duck breasts.

Toad-in-the-Hole with Parsley Batter

The addition of onion and bacon as well as parsley to the batter gives a twist to traditional toad-in-the-hole. Make small individual-sized portions using muffin tins. You will need a wide roasting tin which fits in your oven.

SERVES 4		
	1 small red onion	Freshly milled salt and black pepper
	4 rashers smoked streaky bacon	1 tbsp chopped parsley
	4 large meaty sausages, choose your favourite variety	150ml/¼ pint milk
	2 tbsp olive oil	2 medium eggs
	125g/4½ oz plain flour	

1 Remove the lid from the halogen oven, place the low rack inside the oven and replace the lid. Preheat the halogen oven to 200°C.

2 Finely chop the onion. With scissors, trim the rind from the bacon and cut into thick strips. Cut each sausage into three

3 Arrange the onion, bacon strips and sausage pieces in the dish or roasting tin and drizzle with the oil.

4 Put the dish into the hot oven and cook for 6–8 minutes until the oil is very hot and the bacon and sausages are beginning to brown.

5 Meanwhile, sift the flour, a little seasoning and the parsley into a bowl. Mix the milk with 150ml/¼ pint water. Break the egg into the flour and gradually mix in the milk mixture, beating well to make a smooth batter. Pour the batter into a jug.

6 Remove the lid from the oven and pour the batter over the piping hot sausage mixture. Replace the lid and cook for 25–35 minutes until the batter is puffed up and golden and the sausages are cooked through. Serve immediately.

GOLD STAR STEAK SANDWICH

A big sandwich to take you through the day. Works just as well with chicken, venison or lamb. You will need an oiled baking tray which fits in your oven.

SERVES 1		
	1 gherkin	2 tsp tomato purée
	1 spring onion	Olive oil
	Mayonnaise	1 fillet or sirloin beef steak
	Large handful of rocket leaves	2 tsp wholegrain mustard
	1 garlic clove	Freshly milled salt and black pepper
	2 slices sourdough bread	

1   Remove the lid from the halogen oven, place the high rack inside the oven and replace the lid. Preheat the halogen oven to 220°C.

2   Thinly slice the gherkin and spring onion, put into a small bowl and stir in a little mayonnaise. Tear the rocket leaves if very large.

3   Peel the garlic clove, cut in half and rub the cut side over one side of each piece of bread. Thinly spread with a little tomato purée and drizzle with a little olive oil. Put the bread, coated side uppermost, on the baking tray.

4   Trim the steak and pat dry with kitchen paper. Put the steak on the baking tray, drizzle one side with a little oil, turn the steak over, spread with a little mustard and drizzle over a little oil.

5   Put the tray into the hot oven and cook for about 3–4 minutes each side for a rare steak or longer if you prefer. Remove the bread when it has toasted.

6   When the steak is cooked, cut in half horizontally and put both pieces onto a slice of toasted bread. Season, spoon over the gherkin mixture and add the rocket leaves. Cover with the toasted bread, 'coated side down', and eat whilst hot.

Roast Lamb with Spiced Fennel and Courgette Stuffing

Buy a boned, rolled piece of meat and the hard work is done for you. Just unroll, fill with a tasty stuffing and re-roll. You will need a roasting tin which fits in your oven.

SERVES 4

Stuffing
Few sprigs of rosemary
Small bunch of fresh parsley
2 red chillies (see page 19)
1 garlic clove
1 courgette

1 lemon
2 tsp fennel seeds
Freshly milled salt and black pepper

900g/2 lb boned, rolled shoulder of lamb

1   Remove the lid from the halogen oven, place the low rack inside the oven and replace the lid. Preheat the halogen oven to 190°C.

2   Make the stuffing: pull the rosemary leaves from the stalks and finely chop with the parsley. Cut the chillies in half, remove and discard the seeds and stalk, and finely chop. Crush the garlic and grate the courgette. Grate the rind from the lemon, cut in half and squeeze out the juice. Mix all of these ingredients in a bowl and stir in the fennel seeds and a little seasoning.

3   Unroll the lamb and trim off any excess fat. Spread over the stuffing in a thin layer, then roll the lamb and tie with string into a neat shape.

4   Put the stuffed lamb into the roasting tin and cover with foil. Put into the hot oven and cook for 20 minutes. Turn the lamb over, cover and cook for a further 20 minutes. Again, turn the lamb over, open the foil and cook for a further 10–15 minutes or until browned, piping hot and cooked through. Serve sliced with the pan juices spooned over.

CRUNCHY POLENTA AND SESAME CHICKEN FILLETS

It's so quick and easy to make your own crunchy coated chicken. Add a few chopped herbs or a little ground spice to the coating. Serve with a crisp salad and natural yogurt. You will need an oiled baking tray which fits in your oven.

SERVES 2	2 boneless, skinless chicken breasts	1 tbsp sesame seeds
	1 large egg	Freshly milled white pepper
	4 tbsp polenta	Sunflower oil

1   Remove the lid from the halogen oven, place the high rack inside the oven and replace the lid. Preheat the halogen oven to 200°C.

2   Cut each chicken breast lengthways into three or four mini fillets.

3   Break the egg into a shallow bowl and lightly beat with a fork. Tip the polenta onto a plate and mix in the sesame seeds and a little pepper. Dip the chicken pieces in the beaten egg and then turn the chicken in the polenta coating.

4   Arrange the coated chicken fillets on the oiled baking tray. Put into the hot oven and cook for 15–20 minutes, turning once, until piping hot and cooked through.

SHEPHERD'S PIE

A topsy-turvy dish. I've used carrots and parsnips for the mash rather than putting them with the minced lamb. You will need a large shallow ovenproof dish which fits in your oven.

SERVES 4		
	200g/7 oz parsnips	2 garlic cloves
	200g/7 oz carrots	Small handful of fresh mint leaves
	2 tbsp milk	450g/1 lb lean minced lamb
	2 tbsp butter	400g can crushed tomatoes
	Freshly milled salt and black pepper	2 tbsp liquid vegetable stock
	1 onion	

1   Remove the lid from the halogen oven, place the low rack inside the oven and replace the lid. Preheat the halogen oven to 200°C.

2   Peel the parsnips and the carrots, cut into pieces and cook in boiling water until soft and drain. Whilst still hot, add the milk, butter and a little black pepper, then mash with a potato masher or crush with a fork.

3   Finely chop the onion and crush the garlic. Pull the mint leaves from the stalks and finely chop.

4   Put the mince into the dish and cook in the hot oven for 4–5 minutes until the juices begin to flow. Stir in the onion and cook for 10 minutes until slightly browned and then mix in the garlic, tomatoes, liquid stock and a little seasoning. Cook for a further 25–35 minutes until the mince is cooked and the sauce begins to thicken slightly.

5   Remove the dish from the oven (turn the timer to keep the oven on) and spread a thin layer of mashed parsnip and carrot on top of the mince. Turn up the heat to 250°C and cook for 10 minutes until the mash is piping hot, slightly browned, and cooked through.

Sticky Chicken Wings with Green Salsa

Easy to make with store-cupboard ingredients. Serve with wedges of lime to squeeze over and lots of napkins if you're eating them with your fingers. You will need a large oiled baking tray which fits in your oven.

SERVES 3–4

500g/1 lb 2 oz chicken wings
4 tbsp tomato ketchup
4 tbsp clear honey
2 tbsp Worcestershire sauce
2–3 tsp curry paste
2 tbsp vegetable oil
Freshly milled salt and black pepper

Green Salsa
4 spring onions
1 green pepper
1 lime
Small bunch of parsley
Small bunch of coriander
1 tsp garlic purée
1 tsp chilli paste
2–3 tbsp olive oil

1 Remove the lid from the halogen oven, place the high rack inside the oven and replace the lid. Preheat the halogen oven to 220°C.

2 Trim and discard the wing tips (or use for stock) and cut each in half.

3 In a large bowl mix together the tomato ketchup, honey, Worcestershire sauce, curry paste, oil and seasoning. Tip in the chicken wings and turn in the mix until thoroughly coated. Cover and chill for one to four hours.

4 Make the salsa. Thinly slice the spring onions. Cut the green pepper in half, remove and discard the seeds and stalks, and finely dice. Grate the rind from the lime, cut in half and squeeze the juice. Chop the parsley and coriander.

5 Put all the salsa ingredients into a bowl and season to taste. Cover and chill until needed.

6 Arrange the chicken wings on the tray in a single layer. Put into the hot oven and cook for 8–15 minutes, turning once. Cooking times depend on the size of the wings. Cook until golden, piping hot and cooked through. Serve hot with the salsa.

CAJUN PORK CHOPS WITH ROASTED APPLES

Works equally well with lamb leg steaks or even spareribs. You will need a shallow roasting tin which fits in your oven.

SERVES 3		
	3 pork chops	Pinch chilli powder
	2 eating apples	Pinch cayenne pepper
	1 tsp lemon juice	4 tbsp brown sugar
	2 tsp ground cardamom	Freshly milled black pepper
	2 tsp ground coriander	Vegetable oil

1   Remove the lid from the halogen oven, place the high rack inside the oven and replace the lid. Preheat the halogen oven to 200°C.

2   Snip the pork rind at intervals around the edge to prevent it curling. Core the apples and cut into wedges. Brush with a little lemon juice to prevent browning.

3   In a food (freezer) bag tip in the ground cardamom and coriander, chilli powder, cayenne pepper, sugar and a little black pepper. Add the pork chops and turn them in the spices until thoroughly coated. If there's time, chill for an hour or two to allow the flavours to develop.

4   Put the pork chops and apple wedges into the roasting tin and drizzle over a little oil.

5   Put the roasting tin into the hot oven and cook for 10–15 minutes, turning once – remove the apple wedges if they begin to brown too much. Cook until browned, piping hot and cooked through.

Venison Steaks with Red Wine and Mustard Sauce

A very elegant dish. Venison is lean and healthy, and not as gamey as you might expect. As an alternative use skinless duck breasts. You will need a shallow ovenproof dish which fits in your oven.

SERVES 2	1 tbsp butter	3 tbsp red wine, or red grape juice
	1 tbsp oil	2 tbsp wholegrain mustard
	Freshly milled salt and black pepper	1 tbsp redcurrant or raspberry jelly
	Two 175g/6 oz venison steaks	Salad leaves, to serve

1   Remove the lid from the halogen oven, place the high rack inside the oven and replace the lid. Preheat the halogen oven to 190°C.

2   Put the butter and oil in the dish and place into the hot oven. Lightly season the steaks.

3   When the butter and oil are hot put the steaks into the dish and cook for 3–4 minutes on either side until browned but still pink inside – cook longer if you prefer.

4   Lift the steaks out of the dish, cover with foil and leave to rest in a warm place.

5   Turn the timer on the oven to 6 minutes. Stir the red wine, or red grape juice, wholegrain mustard and redcurrant or raspberry jelly into the pan juices. Put into the hot oven and cook for 2–3 minutes until the sauce is bubbling and piping hot.

6   Pile the leaves onto serving plates. Top with the hot venison steak and spoon over the sauce.

Turkey Escalopes Topped with Lemon, Olives and Walnuts

An escalope is a thin piece of meat or fish which has been flattened. It cooks quickly and is the perfect shape for holding the tasty topping. You will need a large oiled baking tray which fits in your oven.

SERVES 2	2 boneless, skinless turkey slices, about 150g/5½ oz each 1 tbsp plain flour Freshly milled salt and black pepper	Olive oil Small handful of stoned black olives Small handful of chopped walnuts 1 lemon

1 Remove the lid from the halogen oven, place the high rack inside the oven and replace the lid. Preheat the halogen oven to 190°C.

2 Put the turkey slices on a chopping board, cover with clear film and flatten with the end of a rolling pin.

3 Sprinkle the flour onto a plate and stir in a little seasoning. Turn the turkey slices in seasoned flour until lightly coated.

4 Put the turkey escalopes onto the oiled baking tray and drizzle over a little oil. Put into the oven and cook for 10 minutes. Turn them over, drizzle with oil, if needed, return to the oven and cook for 10 minutes.

5 Meanwhile, slice the olives and put into a bowl with the chopped walnuts. Grate over the rind from half the lemon, cut in half and squeeze the juice from the whole fruit and stir in a little seasoning.

6 After 10 minutes, remove the lid from the oven and spoon some of the olive and walnut mixture onto each escalope. Replace the lid and cook for 4–6 minutes until the topping and meat is piping hot and cooked through.

BEEF STRIPS WITH SIZZLING VEGETABLES

All the essential flavours of a stir-fry, plus zingy horseradish. You will need a large shallow roasting tin which fits in your oven.

SERVES 2	1 small red onion	2 fillet or sirloin beef steaks
	½ small red or orange pepper	Sunflower oil
	300g/10½ oz selection of mini vegetables, such as carrots, courgettes, leeks	2 tbsp horseradish sauce
		Freshly milled salt and black pepper

1 Remove the lid from the halogen oven, place the high rack inside the oven and replace the lid. Preheat the halogen oven to 220°C.

2 Quarter the onion and cut into thin slices. Cut the red or orange pepper in half, remove and discard the seeds and stalks, and cut into thin slices. Trim the vegetables and cut into thin strips. Remove any fat from the beef steaks and cut into thin strips.

3 Pour 1 tbsp of the oil into a bowl. Stir in the horseradish sauce, a little seasoning and the strips of beef. Cover and if there's time chill for an hour or two to allow the flavours to develop.

4 Put the vegetables into a food (freezer) bag. Pour in 1 tbsp of the oil and a little seasoning and shake the bag until the vegetables are coated.

5 Tip the vegetables into the roasting tin and push into a single layer. Put into the hot oven and cook for 6–8 minutes until slightly softened and coloured. Arrange the beef on top and cook for 4–6 minutes until, piping hot and cooked through.

Sweet and Sour Pork

A perennial favourite served with rice or noodles. If you like pineapple with your pork, add a small tin of pineapple pieces in natural syrup. You will need a large dish tray which fits in your oven.

SERVES 4		
	450g/1 lb lean pork	1 tsp five-spice powder
	1 red onion	Freshly milled salt and black pepper
	A small piece of fresh root ginger	2 tbsp olive oil
	1 garlic clove	1 chicken stock cube
	6 water chestnuts, optional	1 tbsp clear honey
	Large handful pak choi leaves or Chinese leaves	1 tbsp white wine vinegar
	1 tbsp cornflour	2 tsp light soy sauce

1   Remove the lid from the halogen oven, place the low rack inside the oven. Preheat the halogen oven to 200°C.

2   Trim any excess fat from the pork and cut into thin strips. Finely chop the onion, grate the root ginger and crush the garlic. Slice the water chestnuts, if using, and finely shred the pak choi leaves or Chinese leaves

3   Put the cornflour, five-spice powder and a little seasoning in a food (freezer) bag. Add the strips of pork and shake the bag until the meat is thoroughly coated.

4   Arrange the chopped onion and the coated pork strips in the dish and drizzle over the oil. Put the dish into the hot oven and cook for 6–8 minutes until beginning to brown.

5   Put the kettle on to boil. Crumble the stock cube into a jug and pour over 300ml/½ pint boiling water (from the kettle) and stir in the grated ginger, garlic, honey, vinegar, soy sauce and a little black pepper.

6   Pour the hot stock mix over the browned pork and stir in the shredded pak choi leaves or Chinese leaves and cook for 35–45 minutes, stirring once, until the meat is piping hot and cooked through. Stir in the water chestnuts, if using, 10 minutes before the end of cooking. Cover with a lid or foil if the meat and sauce browns too much.

Pork Chops with Apricot Stuffing

Serve with freshly cooked rice or noodles, and with a little chopped fresh parsley stirred in. You will need a roasting tin which fits in your oven.

SERVES 2

2 red eating apples
3 ready-to-eat dried apricots
1 garlic clove
2 tbsp fresh breadcrumbs
¼ tsp ground allspice
2 tbsp apple juice

Freshly milled salt and black pepper
2 pork chops, about 175g/6 oz, on the bone
Olive oil
2 sprays of tomatoes on the vine (each with 3–4 tomatoes)

1 Remove the lid from the halogen oven, place the low rack inside the oven and replace the lid. Preheat the halogen oven to 190°C.

2 Quarter and core the apples and thinly slice. Finely chop the apricots and crush the garlic.

3 For the stuffing, put the breadcrumbs into a small bowl and stir in the allspice, apple juice, chopped apricots, garlic and a little seasoning.

4 Cut a wide pocket into the side of each pork chop and push some of the stuffing into the cavity.

5 Put the chops into the roasting tin, drizzle with a little oil and put into the hot oven. Cook for 10–12 minutes until golden. Turn the chops over and put the apple wedges and sprays of tomatoes into the tin. Drizzle with oil if necessary and cook for 10–12 minutes until piping hot and the meat is cooked through.

STICKY MARMALADE DUCK

Cooked in the halogen oven, the duck stays very moist. Serve with rice or noodles, or just a large bowlful of salad leaves. You will need a large shallow dish which fits in your oven.

SERVES 4	4 duck legs	2 tsp soy sauce
	¼ small spring cabbage	Freshly milled black pepper
	Small piece of root ginger	2 tsp chicken bouillon powder
	2 tbsp thin-cut marmalade	
	1 tbsp sesame seeds	

1   Remove the lid from the halogen oven, place the low rack inside the oven and replace the lid. Preheat the halogen oven to 200°C.

2   Put the kettle on to boil.

3   Place the duck legs directly onto the low rack and cook for 15 minutes, turning once.

4   Very finely shred the cabbage. Grate the root ginger into a bowl and stir in the marmalade, sesame seeds, soy sauce and black pepper. Put the bouillon powder into a jug and stir in 150ml/¼ pint boiling water (from the kettle).

5   Put the cabbage into the dish and pour over the hot stock. After 15 minutes, remove the lid from the oven, lift out the duck legs and put on top of the cabbage. Spoon over the marmalade mixture, cover with foil and put into the hot oven. Replace the lid and cook for 30–40 minutes until the duck is piping hot and cooked through. Remove the foil for the last 10 minutes to brown the duck.

NUTTY PORK MEATBALLS IN CHILLI TOMATO SAUCE

The peanuts provide texture and crunch, but if you prefer not to use them just add a little extra pork. This dish works well with lean minced beef, lamb or chicken. Serve with hot crispy bread and salad leaves. You need a wide shallow dish which fits your oven.

SERVES 4

Small handful of fresh thyme sprigs or parsley
1 medium egg
55g/2 oz shelled, unsalted peanuts
450g/1 lb lean minced pork
60g/2¼ oz fresh brown breadcrumbs
Freshly milled salt and black pepper
350g/12 oz cherry tomatoes

1 garlic clove
1 medium onion
2 tbsp olive oil
2 tsp bouillon powder
Pinch of sugar
2 tsp chilli sauce

1   Remove the lid from the halogen oven, place the high rack inside the oven and replace the lid. Preheat the oven to 190°C.

2   To make the meatballs, pull the thyme leaves from the stalks and finely chop, or finely chop the parsley. Lightly beat the egg and crush the peanuts.

3   In a large mixing bowl, combine the thyme or parsley, egg, peanuts, pork and breadcrumbs and a little seasoning. Using wetted hands, shape the mixture into 16 small balls.

4   Cut the tomatoes in half, crush the garlic and very finely chop the onion. Put the kettle on to boil.

5   Arrange the meatballs in the dish, add the chopped onion and halved tomatoes, cut side uppermost. Drizzle over the oil.

6   Put into the hot oven and cook for 10–12 minutes, turning once or twice, until the meatballs, onion and tomatoes begin to brown.

7   Put the bouillon powder into a measuring jug and stir in 300ml/½ pint boiling water (from the kettle). Stir in the garlic, sugar, chilli sauce and seasoning.

8   Remove the dish from the oven, replace the lid and set the timer to 5 minutes to keep the oven hot. (It's easier than leaving the dish in the oven.) Pour the stock into the dish around the meatballs. With a fork lightly crush the tomatoes. Cover with foil, return to the oven and cook for 12–15 minutes until meatballs and sauce are cooked through and piping hot.

MUSTARD GLAZED LAMB

Meat is so successful cooked in the halogen oven. Remember to leave it to rest for 10 minutes before carving. You will need a large shallow roasting tin which fits in your oven.

SERVES 4		
	1 tsp ground allspice	2 tbsp sunflower oil
	½ tsp ground ginger	Freshly milled salt and black pepper
	3 tbsp prepared French mustard	950g/2 lb 2 oz boned leg of lamb

1   Remove the lid from the halogen oven, place the low rack inside the oven and replace the lid. Preheat the halogen oven to 190°C.

2   Spoon the ground allspice and ginger, mustard, oil and a little seasoning into a small bowl and mix to a paste.

3   Trim off any excess fat from the lamb. With a sharp knife, make several deep cuts into the meat on all sides.

4   Rub the paste all over the lamb, pushing it into the cuts.

5   Put the lamb into the roasting tin and cover with foil. Put into the hot oven and cook for 20 minutes. Turn the lamb over, cover and cook a further 20 minutes. Again, turn the lamb over, open the foil and cook a further 10–15 minutes or until browned, piping hot and cooked through. Serve sliced with the pan juices spooned over.

TURKEY, RED PEPPER AND CRANBERRY BURGERS

Serve in split burger buns or pitta breads with crisp salad leaves and tomato slices, together with relish, pickles and even a slice of cheese. You will need a flat ovenproof dish which fits in your oven, or use the rack.

SERVES 4–6	1 small red pepper	600g/1 lb 5 oz minced turkey
	12 dried cranberries	Freshly milled salt and black pepper
	Small bunch of parsley	Vegetable oil

1   Remove the lid from the halogen oven, place the low rack inside the oven and replace the lid. Preheat the halogen oven to 220°C.

2   Cut the red pepper in half, remove and discard the seeds and stalk. Finely chop the red pepper, cranberries and parsley.

3   Put the minced turkey into a mixing bowl and add a little seasoning. Tip in the chopped red pepper, cranberries and parsley. With a fork, mix together well.

4   With wetted hands, divide and shape the mixture into large or small burgers and brush with a little oil.

5   Put the burgers into the dish or directly onto the rack in the hot oven. Cook for 4–6 minutes until browned, turn over and cook for 3–4 on the other side until browned, piping hot and cooked through.

PHEASANT CASSEROLE WITH ORANGE, CORIANDER AND SLICED POTATO TOPPING

Game is more widely available these days from butchers and from supermarkets, and it comes in more convenient cuts. Serve with redcurrant jelly. You will need a large dish which fits in your oven.

SERVES 4		
	2 shallots	Freshly milled salt and black pepper
	1 orange	2 tbsp olive oil
	2 rashers streaky bacon	150ml/¼ pint dry cider
	4 boneless pheasant breasts, skinned	300ml/½ pint chicken stock
	2 tbsp plain flour	300g/10½ oz potatoes
	1 tsp ground coriander	55g/2 oz butter, melted

1　Remove the lid from the halogen oven, place the low rack inside the oven and replace the lid. Preheat the halogen oven to 200°C.

2　Finely chop the shallots. Finely grate the rind from the orange, cut in half and squeeze out the juice. With scissors, trim the rind from the bacon and cut into thick strips. Cut the pheasant into bite-sized pieces.

3　Put the flour, coriander and seasoning into a food (freezer) bag. Add the pieces of pheasant and shake the bag until thoroughly coated.

4　Arrange the shallots, bacon strips and coated pheasant pieces in the dish and drizzle with the oil.

5　Put into the hot oven and cook for 6–8 minutes until beginning to brown.

6　Put the orange rind and juice, cider and stock into a small saucepan and bring to the boil. Stir into the browned ingredients and cover. Cook for 50 minutes, stirring occasionally until the meat is tender.

7　Meanwhile, peel and thinly slice the potatoes. Cook in boiling salted water until tender – don't overcook them or they will collapse – and drain.

8　After 50 minutes, remove the lid from the oven. Uncover the dish and arrange the cooked potato slices on top of the meat. Drizzle over the melted butter and cook for 10–15 minutes until piping hot and cooked through.

4.   FISHY THINGS

SHELLFISH, WHITE FISH AND OILY FISH – the harvest of the deep – contain so much aquatic goodness and offer so much variety that it really does make sense to sample as many types of sustainable seafood as you can.

Fish is always recommended as an essential part of any healthy, balanced diet. Trout, for example, is a great alternative to meat, being full of protein, relatively low in fat and an excellent source of essential fish oil. All kinds of fish (including mackerel, sardines and salmon, which are featured in this chapter) are highly beneficial. Cooking times are generally quicker than for meat dishes, and fish dishes tend to have a lighter character.

It is good to know just how many exciting and flavourful things can be done with seafood. Here is a set of recipes to demonstrate just how adaptable fish dishes can be, ranging from Fish Kebabs with Mango Salsa (page 112) and Skate Wings with Capers and Prawns (page 124) to Roasted Fish with Spiced Potatoes and Peas (page 123) and Salmon Fishcakes with Watercress Dressing (page 114).

A fish fiesta from your halogen oven.

MUSTARD SARDINES

The wholegrain mustard marinade adds a gentle heat to the sardines. Serve a mixed salad and hot bread alongside the spring onion yogurt dressing for a light meal. You will need a shallow baking tray or roasting tin which fits your oven.

SERVES 4

1 small spring onion
2 small lemons
Small handful of fresh parsley
2 tbsp olive oil
2 tbsp wholegrain mustard

Freshly milled salt and pepper
8 fresh sardines, gutted
300ml/½ pint natural yogurt
A little milk, optional

1   Remove the lid from the halogen oven, place the high rack inside the oven and replace the lid.

2   Finely chop the spring onion. Grate the rind from one of the lemons, cut in half and squeeze out the juice. Cut the second lemon into wedges and finely chop the parsley

3   Prepare the marinade: pour the olive oil into a large non-metallic bowl. Stir in the wholegrain mustard, lemon rind and juice, half of the chopped parsley and a little seasoning.

4   Put the sardines into the marinade and turn each one until thoroughly coated. Arrange them in a single layer, cover and chill for an hour.

5   Prepare the dressing: pour the yogurt into a small bowl. Stir in the chopped spring onion and season to taste (if it is too thick stir in a little cold water or milk).

6   Preheat the halogen oven to 200°C.

7   Lift the sardines from the marinade onto the baking tray or roasting tin and arrange in a single layer. Drizzle over any remaining marinade.

8   Put into the hot oven and cook for 12–15 minutes, turning once until browned and cooked through. (The time will depend on the size of the sardines.) Sprinkle over the remaining parsley and serve hot or cold with the lemon wedges and yogurt dressing.

FISH KEBABS WITH MANGO SALSA

Curry can overpower fish, but korma is a lighter, fragrant style of curry and the salsa is very cooling. Serve with poppadoms and rice. You will need four metal skewers and a baking tray which fits in your oven.

SERVES 2

8 button mushrooms
1 green pepper
400g/14 oz skinless firm fish fillets, such as salmon,
    monkfish or hake
Small piece of root ginger
2 tsp korma curry paste
150ml/¼ pint natural yogurt
1 tbsp olive oil

Freshly milled white pepper

Salsa
1 small mango
¼ cucumber
4 mint leaves
2 tbsp dry white wine (optional)

1   Trim the mushroom stalks level with the base of the caps. Cut the pepper in half, remove and discard the seeds and stalk, and cut into 8 pieces. Trim the fish and cut into sixteen bite-sized pieces.

2   Prepare the marinade: grate the root ginger into a wide shallow non-metallic bowl and stir in the curry paste, yogurt, oil and a little white pepper.

3   Thread the pieces of fish, mushroom and pepper onto the skewers, leaving a small gap between each piece. Cover and chill for an hour.

4   Prepare the salsa: peel the mango and cut the flesh away from the stone. Peel the cucumber, cut in half lengthways and scoop out the seeds.

5   Finely chop the mango flesh, cucumber and mint leaves, or use a food processor and put into a small bowl. Stir in the wine or water and season to taste with white pepper.

6   Remove the lid from the oven, place the high rack inside the oven and replace the lid. Preheat the halogen oven to 190°C.

7   Lift the kebabs from the marinade onto the baking tray and spoon over any remaining marinade.

8   Put into the hot oven and cook for 12–18 minutes, turning once, until browned and cooked through. (The time will depend on the thickness of the fish.) Serve hot with the salsa.

SPICED SEAFOOD WITH RICE NOODLES

The addition of rice noodles makes a complete meal. Bags of frozen seafood are a useful standby, as is a range of spices. You will need a large ovenproof dish which fits in your oven.

SERVES 2–3

300g/10½ oz mixed, shelled shellfish, no need to thaw if frozen
2 tbsp wholegrain mustard
2 tsp Worcestershire sauce
Small pinch of cayenne pepper

300ml/½ pint fish or vegetable stock
1 tbsp olive oil
1 tbsp chopped parsley
Freshly milled black pepper
100g/3½ oz rice noodles

1   Remove the lid from the halogen oven, place the low rack inside the oven and replace the lid. Preheat the halogen oven to 200°C. Put the kettle on to boil.

2   Put the shellfish into the dish and stir in the wholegrain mustard, Worcestershire sauce, cayenne pepper, fish or vegetable stock, olive oil, chopped parsley and a little black pepper.

3   Cover, and put into the hot oven. Cook for 15–18 minutes until just cooked.

4   Put the noodles into a large bowl, pour over boiling water from the kettle to cover and stand for 10 minutes. Drain well and stir into the cooked seafood. Cover and cook for 4–6 minutes until piping hot.

Salmon Fishcakes with Watercress Dressing

Using both unsmoked and smoked fish gives a rich flavour to these fishcakes; they also freeze well. Cook from frozen. You will need a greased baking tray which fits in your oven.

MAKES 8
small fishcakes

350g/12 oz potatoes
Freshly milled salt and black pepper
250g/9 oz skinless salmon fillet
100g/3½ oz smoked salmon pieces
2 spring onions
1 tsp chopped parsley
1 medium egg

3 tbsp fresh white breadcrumbs

Dressing
4 walnut halves
Small bunch watercress
150ml/¼ pint olive oil
2 tbsp lemon juice

1   Peel the potatoes, cut into pieces and cook in boiling salted water until soft. Drain, mash, and leave to cool.

2   Remove any bones from the fresh and smoked salmon. Either cut the fish and spring onions very finely, or use a food processor, but don't mix to a pulp.

3   Put the mashed potato into a large bowl and mix in the chopped fish and spring onions, chopped parsley and a little seasoning.

4   Divide the mixture into eight and shape each portion into flat round cakes.

5   Break the egg into a shallow bowl and lightly beat with a fork. Tip the breadcrumbs onto a plate. Turn the fishcakes in the beaten egg and coat with the crumbs. Chill for 15 minutes to 'firm' up.

6   Remove the lid from the halogen oven, place the low rack inside the oven and replace the lid. Preheat the halogen oven to 200°C.

7   Finely chop the walnuts, pull the leaves from the watercress stalks and finely chop. Pour the oil and lemon juice into a small bowl and whisk with a fork. Stir in the chopped walnuts, watercress and seasoning to taste.

8   Arrange the fish cakes on the greased baking tray. Put into the hot oven and cook for 15 minutes, turning once until cooked through and golden. Serve piping hot with the dressing.

ITALIAN TROUT

This healthy dish is full of Italian flavours: fresh aromatic oregano, black olives and plum tomatoes. You will need an ovenproof dish which fits in your oven.

SERVES 2

2 shallots
Small handful of mange-touts
6 medium Italian tomatoes
4 stoned black olives
4 skinless trout fillets

1 tbsp olive oil
2 tsp lemon juice
Pinch of sugar
1 tbsp freshly chopped oregano
Freshly milled salt and black pepper

1   Remove the lid from the halogen oven, place the low rack inside the oven and replace the lid. Preheat the halogen oven to 200°C.

2   Finely chop the shallots. Cut the mange-touts into thin strips. Roughly chop the tomatoes and slice the olives. Cut the fish into thin strips, removing any bones.

3   Put the shallots and oil into the dish. Put into the hot oven and cook for 5–8 minutes until beginning to soften.

4   Stir in the tomatoes, lemon juice, sugar, mange-touts, olives, oregano and two tablespoons of water. Return to the oven and cook for 12 minutes, stirring once until the vegetables are almost cooked. (If too dry add a little boiling water.)

5   Mix in the strips of trout, return to the oven and cook for 10–12 minutes until piping hot and cooked through. Season if necessary.

THAI SEAFISH AND PRAWNS

Lemon grass gives a sweet-sour flavour and lovely fragrance to Thai-style food and is available fresh or dry. It looks a bit like a spring onion. Cut into slices or, as here, bruise with the back of a knife. You will need a large ovenproof dish which fits in your oven.

SERVES 4		
	400g/14 oz boneless fish fillet, such as salmon, trout or coley	150ml/¼ pint coconut milk
	¼ cos lettuce	150ml/¼ pint fish or vegetable stock
	1 red chilli (see page 19)	100g/3½ oz shelled prawns
	Small piece of lemon grass	4 flatbreads
	Small piece of root ginger	Freshly milled salt and black pepper

1   Remove the lid from the halogen oven, place the low rack inside the oven and replace the lid. Preheat the halogen oven to 190°C.

2   Cut the fish into small bite-sized pieces, removing any bones. Finely slice the cos lettuce. Cut the chilli in half, remove and discard the seeds and stalk. Bruise the lemon grass by tapping it with the back of a knife. Finely grate the root ginger.

3   Pour the coconut milk and stock into a small pan and bring just to the boil.

4   Put the fish and prawns into the dish, then stir in the sliced lettuce, two pieces of chilli, lemon grass and the grated ginger. Pour over the hot coconut milk and stock and stir to mix.

5   Cover, and put into the hot oven on the low rack. Put the high rack in place and cook for 15–18 minutes until piping hot and cooked through.

6   Wrap the flatbreads in foil and put on the high rack for the last 3–5 minutes' cooking time.

7   Remove the lemon grass and two pieces of chilli and season to taste before serving with the flatbreads.

Whole Stuffed Fish Roasted with Almonds

Mushroom, spinach and dill is my choice of stuffing, but try breadcrumbs, fennel and watercress leaves for a change. You will need a large roasting tin which fits in your oven.

SERVES 3–4

100g/3½ oz mushrooms
2 tbsp sunflower oil
Large handful of spinach leaves
Small bunch of dill
1 lime

Freshly milled black pepper
Large whole fish, such as sea bass or salmon, gutted, about 900g/2 lb
55g/2 oz flaked almonds

1   Remove the lid from the halogen oven, place the low rack inside the oven and replace the lid. Preheat the halogen oven to 200°C.

2   Prepare the stuffing: finely chop the mushrooms and put into the roasting tray with 1 tbsp of the oil. Put into the hot oven and cook for 6–8 minutes until the mushrooms are beginning to sizzle. Remove from the oven and spoon the mushrooms into a bowl.

3   Thinly shred the spinach leaves and dill. Grate the rind from the lime, cut in half and squeeze out the juice. Stir them all into the bowl of mushrooms and add a little black pepper.

4   Spoon the stuffing into the body cavity of the fish. Carefully lift the fish into the roasting tin. Make three or four diagonal cuts on the side of the fish, drizzle over the remaining oil and scatter over the almonds.

5   Cover and cook in the hot oven for 40–55 minutes until piping hot and cooked through, but start looking to see if it is cooked from 35 minutes onwards. (The time will depend on the thickness of the fish.) Remove the cover for the last 15 minutes.

FISH PIE WITH SWEET POTATO MASH

Sweet potatoes are often overlooked as a topping in place of traditional mash. They cook more quickly than potatoes, are a fabulous orange colour and give a little spice and sweetness to the dish. You will need a large shallow ovenproof dish which fits in your oven.

SERVES 4

300g/10½ oz sweet potatoes
2 tbsp milk
2 tbsp butter
Freshly milled black pepper
1 green pepper
400g can crushed tomatoes

200g carton low-fat crème fraîche
Large handful of spinach leaves
½ tbsp fennel seeds
4 thin skinless fish fillets, about 115g/4 oz each
1 tbsp olive oil

1   Remove the lid from the halogen oven, place the low rack inside the oven and replace the lid. Preheat the halogen oven to 200°C.

2   Peel the sweet potatoes, cut into pieces and cook in boiling water until soft and drain. Whilst still hot, add the milk, butter and black pepper, then mash with a potato masher or crush with a fork.

3   Cut the pepper in half, remove and discard the seeds and stalk, and very finely chop.

4   Put the chopped pepper into the dish and pour over the tomatoes and crème fraîche. Stir in the spinach leaves, fennel seeds and a little black pepper.

5   Put into the hot oven and cook for 20–25 minutes until the sauce begins to thicken slightly and the peppers soften.

6   Remove the dish from the oven (turn the timer to keep the oven on) and lay the fillets on top of the sauce. Drizzle over the oil and cook for 12–15 minutes until the fish is just cooked. As before, remove from the oven and spread a thin layer of mashed sweet potato on top of the fish. Turn up the heat to 250°C and cook for 10 minutes until the mash is piping hot, slightly browned and cooked through.

POACHED SALMON WITH SHREDDED VEGETABLES

A parcel of vegetables steams on the low rack whilst the salmon poaches in wine, lemon and stock on the high rack. You will need foil or two large shallow ovenproof dishes which fit in your oven.

SERVES 4

2 carrots
2 courgettes
1 small fennel bulb
1 small red onion
1 lemon

Small bunch of parsley
Freshly milled black pepper
150ml/¼ pint vegetable stock
4 thick salmon fillets, about 150g/5½ oz each
2 tbsp dry white wine (optional)

1   Remove the lid from the halogen oven, place the low rack inside the oven and replace the lid. Preheat the halogen oven to 200°C.

2   Finely shred the carrots, courgettes, fennel and onion into thin shreds. Slice the lemon and finely chop the parsley.

3   Put the shredded vegetables onto a large piece of foil, or into one of the dishes. Pour over half of the stock, add a lemon slice and a little seasoning.

4   Gather up the foil, seal the parcel securely, or cover the dish with a lid or foil. Put into the hot oven and cook for 30 minutes.

5   Meanwhile, put the salmon fillets onto a large piece of foil, or into the second dish. Pour over the remaining stock, wine (or water), add the lemon slices and a little seasoning.

6   After 25 minutes, remove the lid from the oven. Put in the high rack, the salmon dish on top, and replace the lid. Cook for a further 20 minutes until piping hot and cooked through. Serve the salmon on top of the vegetables and spoon over the juices.

Roasted Fish with Spiced Potatoes and Peas

This is my version of fish and chips, plus a dollop of tomato ketchup. You will need foil and a baking tray which fits in your oven.

SERVES 2

400g/14 oz potatoes
2 tbsp sunflower oil
1 tsp ground cumin or coriander
Freshly milled salt and black pepper
200g/7 oz frozen peas

1 tsp mint sauce
150g/5½ oz plain tacos
1 small egg
2 thick white fish fillets, about 150g/5½ oz each
Tomato ketchup, to serve

1. Remove the lid from the halogen oven, take out the low and high racks from inside the oven and replace the lid. Preheat the halogen oven to 200°C.

2. Peel the potatoes and cut into even bite-sized pieces. Pour 1 tbsp of the oil into a large bowl, add the cumin or coriander and black pepper (add a little salt if necessary) and potato pieces and mix until coated.

3. Spoon the coated potatoes over the base of the hot oven and cook for 25–40 minutes (depending on the size), stirring occasionally until almost roasted and cooked through.

4. Meanwhile, put the peas and mint sauce onto a large piece of foil. Pour over 2 tbsp water and gather up the foil to seal the parcel securely.

5. Put the tacos in a food (freezer) bag and crush until quite fine, then tip onto a plate. Break the egg into a shallow bowl and lightly beat with a fork. Turn the fish fillets in the beaten egg and coat with the taco crumbs.

6. Put the fish and parcel of peas onto the baking tray.

7. After the 25–40 minutes' cooking remove the lid from the oven. Put in the high rack and tray, replace the lid and cook for 8–12 minutes, turning the fish once, until the fish and peas are piping hot and cooked through and the potatoes are roasted. Serve with tomato ketchup.

Skate Wings with Capers and Prawns

Skate is my favourite fish, it needs almost no effort to prepare yet looks very elegant. Use all capers or all prawns if you prefer, but I like a combination of the two. Just halve the recipe for one serving. You will need a large shallow ovenproof dish which fits in your oven.

SERVES 2

1 tbsp capers in brine
1 lemon
70g/2½ oz shelled prawns

55g/2 oz butter
2 small skate wings
Freshly milled black pepper

1   Remove the lid from the halogen oven, place the high rack inside the oven and replace the lid. Preheat the halogen oven to 190°C.

2   Rinse and drain the capers. Finely grate the rind from the lemon, cut in half and squeeze the juice. Put the lemon rind and juice, capers and prawns into a small bowl.

3   Put the butter into a small bowl, put into the hot oven and leave for a few seconds, watching carefully until it has melted.

4   Pour half of the melted butter into the dish, put the skate wings side by side on top and pour over the remaining butter. Sprinkle with black pepper.

5   Put into the hot oven and cook for 4–6 minutes until cooked. With a fish slice carefully turn the skate over, sprinkle with black pepper again, and cook for another 4 minutes. Spoon the prawn and caper mixture over the skate and cook for 2–4 minutes until piping hot and cooked through (the time will depend on the thickness of the skate). If the hot moving air causes the prawns and capers to move, put the high rack upside down on top of the fish. Serve immediately.

Crunchy Herb-Topped Salmon Fillets

Crushed tortilla chips add crunch to the sorrel and mushroom topping. Crisps or poppadums work just as well. You will need a large, shallow buttered ovenproof dish which fits in your oven.

SERVES 4

8 tortilla chips
6 button mushrooms
Small bunch of sorrel or flat-leaved parsley
Freshly milled salt and black pepper

4 thick salmon fillets, about 150g/5½ oz each
Vegetable oil
1 tbsp grated Parmesan cheese

1   Remove the lid from the halogen oven, place the high rack inside the oven and replace the lid. Preheat the halogen oven to 200°C

2   With a rolling pin, crush the tortilla chips. Finely chop the mushrooms. Pull the sorrel or parsley leaves from the stalks and finely chop.

3   Put the chopped mushrooms into a small bowl and stir in the chopped sorrel or parsley and a little seasoning.

4   Put the salmon fillets into the dish and brush with a little oil. Press some of the mushroom and herb mixture on top of each one. Sprinkle over the crushed taco shells and the Parmesan cheese.

5   Put the dish into the hot oven and cook for 10–15 minutes until lightly browned, piping hot and cooked through.

SEAFOOD AND SWEETCORN CRUMBLE

Crumble mixes are very useful for all types of savoury dishes. Keep a quantity in the freezer, with or without cheese, and add a few chopped herbs or nuts before use. You will need a large ovenproof dish and a baking tray which fit in your oven.

SERVES 4

1 garlic clove
4 spring onions
350g/12 oz mixed skinless seafood, such as salmon, coley, prawns
227g can crushed tomatoes
175g/6 oz frozen sweetcorn
1 tsp chopped fresh fennel leaves
Freshly milled salt and black pepper

Crumble topping
115g/4 oz plain wholemeal flour
55g/2 oz butter
55g/2 oz hard cheese, such as Cheddar, Red Leicester, Parmesan

1. Remove the lid from the halogen oven, place the low rack inside the oven and replace the lid. Preheat the halogen oven to 200°C.

2. Crush the garlic clove and finely slice the spring onions. Cut the seafood into bite-sized pieces.

3. Stir the garlic, spring onions, tomatoes and sweetcorn into the dish. Put into the hot oven and cook for 20 minutes, stirring occasionally until slightly thickened.

4. For the topping, tip the flour into a large bowl. Cut the butter into small pieces and add to the flour. Using your fingertips, rub the butter into the mix until it resembles coarse crumbs. Grate the cheese into the bowl and mix in.

5. Sprinkle the topping evenly over the baking tray.

6. Stir the seafood, chopped fennel and a little seasoning into the tomato mixture, and put back into the oven.

7. After 20 minutes, remove the lid from the oven. Put the high rack and baking tray of crumble into the oven and replace the lid, cook for 15–18 minutes until the fish is cooked through and the crumble is lightly browned.

8. Serve portions of the seafood and sweetcorn topped with the crumble.

Seared Mackerel with Chilli, Lemon and Parsley

The heat from the element in the halogen oven sears and crisps the skin of rich oily mackerel just like a barbecue. You will need a large shallow ovenproof dish which fits in your oven.

SERVES 2

1 small lemon
1 red chilli (see page 10)
Small bunch of parsley

2 mackerel
2 tsp olive oil
Freshly milled salt and black pepper

1   Remove the lid from the halogen oven, place the high rack inside the oven and replace the lid. Preheat the halogen oven to 220°C.

2   Finely grate the rind from the lemon, cut in half and squeeze the juice. Cut the chilli in half, remove and discard the seeds and stalk and finely chop. Pull the parsley leaves from the stalks.

3   Wash the fish under running cold water and dry with kitchen paper. With a sharp knife make three or four diagonal cuts on each side of the fish.

4   Put a quarter of the chopped parsley and the lemon rind in the body cavity of each fish and lift into the dish. In a small bowl mix together the lemon juice, chopped chilli, oil and a little seasoning. Spoon the mixture over each fish.

5   Put the dish into the hot oven and cook for 12–18 minutes, turning once, until browned, crisp and cooked through (the time will depend on the size of the mackerel).

Smoked Mackerel Pots

Horseradish is a good accompaniment to oily, strong-flavoured fish like mackerel. Serve with a crisp salad and hot crunchy bread. You will need two greased ovenproof dishes the size of cereal bowls which fit in your oven.

SERVES 2

250g/9 oz cooked smoked mackerel
4 tomatoes
100g/3½ oz Cheddar cheese
½ lemon
½–1 tsp horseradish sauce

2 tbsp fish or vegetable stock
Freshly milled salt and black pepper
2 small courgettes
1 tbsp olive oil

1. Remove the lid from the halogen oven, place the low rack inside the oven and replace the lid. Preheat the halogen oven to 190°C.

2. Skin and flake the mackerel, removing any bones. Finely chop the tomatoes. Finely grate the cheese. Squeeze the juice from the lemon.

3. Put the flaked fish into a small bowl and stir in the tomatoes, a third of the cheese, the lemon juice, horseradish sauce, fish or vegetable stock and a little seasoning. Divide the mixture between the two dishes.

4. Grate the courgettes into a bowl and stir in the remaining cheese, oil and a little seasoning. Spoon on top of the fish mixture, spread out to cover the surface and press down.

5. Cover with foil and cook in the hot oven for 20 minutes. Remove the foil and cook for a further 10–15 minutes until piping hot and cooked through.

BAKED TROUT FILLETS WITH TOMATOES, PEPPERS AND OREGANO

A complete meal in a dish. Just serve with hot crusty bread and a glass of wine. You will need an ovenproof dish which fits in your oven.

SERVES 2

1 small red pepper
1 small yellow pepper
1 garlic clove
1 small red onion
8 cherry tomatoes
Small bunch of oregano
1 tbsp olive oil

2 tbsp capers
150 ml/¼ pint fish or vegetable stock
2 tbsp dry vermouth
Freshly milled salt and black pepper
4 trout fillets
Small handful baby spinach leaves

1   Remove the lid from the halogen oven, place the low rack inside the oven and replace the lid. Preheat the halogen oven to 200°C.

2   Cut the red and yellow peppers in half, remove and discard the seeds and stalks, and thinly slice. Crush the garlic and finely chop the red onion. Quarter the tomatoes. Pull the oregano leaves from the stalks.

3   Put the oil, onion, garlic and red and yellow peppers into the dish. Put into the hot oven and cook for 5–8 minutes until beginning to soften.

4   Lift the dish out of the oven, replace the lid and set the timer for 30 minutes. Stir in the oregano, tomatoes, capers, stock, vermouth and a little seasoning. Return to the oven and cook for 6–8 minutes until bubbling.

5   Remove the dish from the oven and replace the lid. Put the trout fillets on top of the dish and scatter over spinach leaves.

6   Cover the dish loosely with foil. Put the dish back into the hot oven and cook for 10–12 minutes until piping hot and cooked through.

HOT PRAWNS WITH NOODLES

If using shelled prawns or other seafood instead of trout the quantity will be 300g/10½ oz. You will need a large shallow ovenproof dish which fits in your oven.

SERVES 2–3

½ cucumber
Small bunch of coriander
250g/9 oz dried egg noodles
1 tbsp sunflower oil
400g/14 oz raw tiger prawns in their shells, thawed if
    frozen

2 tbsp pine nuts
1 tbsp fish or vegetable bouillon powder
Freshly milled salt and black pepper

1   Remove the lid from the halogen oven, place the high rack inside the oven and replace the lid. Preheat the halogen oven to 220°C.

2   Peel the cucumber, cut in half along the length and scoop out the seeds with a spoon. Cut into 1cm/½ inch slices. Finely chop the coriander leaves.

3   Put the kettle on to boil. With the boiling water, cook the noodles according to the packet instructions and drain.

4   Pour the oil into the dish and stir in the sliced cucumber, prawns and pine nuts. Put into the hot oven and cook for 6–8 minutes until the prawns are just beginning to change colour.

5   Put the bouillon powder and a little seasoning into a jug and stir in 150ml/¼ pint boiling water.

6   Remove the lid from the oven and carefully stir the stock and chopped coriander into the dish – if you prefer, remove the dish from the oven. Replace the lid, and set the timer for 8 minutes. Cook until the prawns are piping hot and cooked through. Serve with the hot drained noodles.

Roasted Fish with Stuffed Mushrooms

Polenta, made from cornmeal, is a quick and easy coating, especially good for skinless pieces of fish or shelled shellfish. Just shake it over. You will need a shallow dish and a greased baking tray which fits in your oven.

SERVES 4

4 large flat-cap mushrooms
55g/2 oz fresh white breadcrumbs
1 tbsp chopped unsalted peanuts
1 tsp chilli sauce
Freshly milled salt and black pepper

1 tbsp grated Parmesan cheese, or Cheddar
2 tbsp olive oil
100g/3½ oz polenta
4 thick boned, skinless white fish steaks or fillets,
    about 150g/5½ oz each

1   Remove the lid from the halogen oven, place the low rack inside the oven and replace the lid. Preheat the halogen oven to 200°C.

2   Wipe the mushrooms with damp kitchen paper. Remove and finely chop the stalks, leaving the caps whole.

3   Tip the breadcrumbs into a small bowl and stir in the mushroom stalks, peanuts and chilli sauce and a little seasoning. Put the mushrooms into the dish and spoon the filling into the caps. Sprinkle over the cheese and drizzle with a little oil.

4   Cook in the hot oven for 12–15 minutes.

5   Put the polenta and seasoning into a food (freezer) bag, shake to mix, add the fish steaks, or fillets, one at a time, and gently shake until thoroughly coated.

6   Arrange the coated pieces of fish onto the tray, drizzle with a little of the oil.

7   Remove the lid from the oven. Put in the high rack and tray and replace the lid. Cook for 12–18 minutes, turning once until piping hot and cooked through. (The time will depend on the size of the fish.) Serve the fish with the stuffed mushrooms.

CRUMBED FISH FINGERS

With their irregular shapes these fish fingers are certainly home-made. Serve in wraps with salad and mayonnaise. You will need a flat baking tray which fits in your oven.

SERVES 3–4

400g/14 oz skinless, fish fillet – choose a thick piece, such as salmon, pollock or tuna
2 tbsp plain flour
1 large egg
1 tbsp olive oil

6 tbsp fine white breadcrumbs
1 tbsp chopped parsley
1 tsp grated lemon rind
Freshly milled salt and black pepper

1   Remove the lid from the halogen oven, place the high rack inside the oven and replace the lid. Preheat the halogen oven to 200°C.

2   Cut the fish into finger-length strips about 2.5cm/1 inch wide and 2.5cm/1 inch deep. Remove any bones from the fish and pat dry with kitchen paper.

3   Spoon the flour onto a plate. Break the egg into a shallow dish and beat with the oil. Tip the breadcrumbs onto a large plate and mix in the chopped parsley, lemon rind and a little seasoning.

4   Dust each fish finger with a little flour. Using tongs or two forks, dip each piece into the egg, allowing excess egg to drip off, then coat with the herby crumb mixture. Repeat using the remaining flour, egg and crumbs and lift them onto the tray. If there's time chill for 15 minutes to let the coating firm up.

5   Put the tray into the hot oven and cook for 6–8 minutes until browned, crisp and cooked through. Turn the fish fingers over and cook for 1–2 minutes to crisp the other side.

Sea Bass with Herb Stuffing

Remember – when buying whole fish it has to fit into the halogen oven. Serve with lemon wedges to squeeze over. You will need a large shallow ovenproof dish which fits in your oven.

SERVES 1

1 small lime
2 small spring onions
Small bunch of tarragon
2 sprigs of rocket leaves

1 sea bass
Vegetable oil
Freshly milled salt and black pepper

1   Remove the lid from the halogen oven, place the high rack inside the oven and replace the lid. Preheat the halogen oven to 200°C.

2   Cut the lime in half, thinly slice one half and save the other half to squeeze over the cooked fish. Cut the spring onions into shreds. Pull the tarragon and rocket leaves from the stalks.

3   Wash the fish under running cold water and dry with kitchen paper. With a sharp knife make three or four diagonal cuts on each side of the fish.

4   Put the lime slices along the length of the body cavity and fill with the shredded spring onions, tarragon and rocket leaves. Lift into the dish. Brush with oil and season.

5   Put the dish into the hot oven and cook for 12–18 minutes, turning once, until browned and cooked through (the time will depend on the size of the sea bass).

Roasted Mackerel with Beetroots and Crème Fraîche Sauce

Mackerel is an oily, dark-fleshed fish, perfect for roasting with just a simple coating of fine oatmeal. It is available all year round. You will need a shallow ovenproof dish and a roasting tray which fits in your oven.

SERVES 4

1 red onion
8 small cooked, peeled beetroot
2 tbsp freshly chopped parsley
2 tbsp unsweetened orange juice
150ml/¼ pint crème fraîche

150ml/¼ pint vegetable stock
Freshly milled salt and black pepper
4 mackerel, gutted and heads removed
2–3 tbsp fine oatmeal
2 tbsp olive oil

1   Remove the lid from the halogen oven, place the low rack inside the oven and replace the lid. Preheat the halogen oven to 200°C.

2   Finely chop the onion, and slice each beetroot in half.

3   Put the onion, beetroot halves and chopped parsley into the shallow dish. Stir in the orange juice, crème fraîche, stock and a little seasoning.

4   Cover and cook in the hot oven for 25 minutes.

5   Meanwhile, wash the fish under running cold water and dry with kitchen paper. With a sharp knife make three or four diagonal cuts on each side of the fish.

6   Sprinkle the oatmeal onto a large plate and stir in a little black pepper. Brush the fish with a little oil and roll in the oatmeal to coat. Arrange the fish on the tray.

7   After 25 minutes, remove the lid from the oven. Put in the high rack and tray of fish and cook for 12–15 minutes, turning once, until browned and cooked through (the time will depend on the size of the mackerel). Serve the fish with the beetroots and sauce.

5. Sweet and Sticky Desserts

Sweet and sticky desserts — what a treat! Indulge in a little of what you like, and invite friends or family to share in the delights.

You will find your halogen oven handles all these inviting recipes with ease. In fact it is just the thing for cheesecake and crumble, puddings and tarts. All the desserts here are deliciously sweet; some of them are stickier than others. To get really stuck in try Sticky Date and Cherry Upside-Down Pudding (page 141), Sticky Roasted Pineapple and Oranges with Pancakes (page 155), Baked Cranberry Stuffed Apples (page 140), or for something smoother there are recipes for Blueberry and Strawberry Brioche Pudding (page 160) or Chocolate and Raspberry Delight (page 151).

Whichever desserts you choose, you can be sure to round off your meal in the most captivating way.

BAKED CRANBERRY STUFFED APPLES

Walnuts, dried apricots and cranberries with a hint of spice make a delicious filling. Bramley apples soften and begin to collapse when baked, but you can use eating apples. Serve hot or warm with custard, plain Greek yogurt or vanilla ice cream. You will need a shallow ovenproof dish which fits in your oven.

SERVES 4

4 small Bramley apples
60g/2¼ oz walnut pieces
3 dried ready-to-eat dried apricots
2 tbsp ready-to-eat dried cranberries

3 tbsp demerara sugar
2 tbsp soft butter
¼ tsp ground mixed spice

1 Remove the lid from the halogen oven, place the low rack inside the oven and replace the lid. Preheat the oven to 190°C.

2 With a corer or a small sharp knife remove the apple cores. Score a line round the middle of each apple, cutting just through the skin.

3 Roughly chop the walnut pieces, apricots and cranberries. Put them in a bowl, add the sugar, butter, and mixed spice, and mix thoroughly.

4 With a small spoon push this mixture into the cavity in each apple, pressing down to pack as much in as possible.

5 Arrange them in the dish and pour round 2 tbsp cold water.

6 Put into the hot oven and cook for 20–25 minutes or until the apples are soft and starting to collapse, but still just holding their shape.

Sticky Date and Cherry Upside-Down Pudding

It's always a delight to turn this type of pudding out onto a plate and see the pattern of the fruits which are now on the top. Serve with custard, cream or crème fraîche. You will need a buttered base-lined 20cm/8 inch deep ovenproof dish which fits in your oven.

SERVES 6–8	1 lime	1 tsp ground mixed spice
	200g/7 oz stoned dates	2 medium eggs
	9 glacé cherries	115g/4 oz butter, plus extra for greasing
	140g/5 oz light brown caster sugar	2 tbsp milk
	175g/6 oz self-raising flour	

1   Remove the lid from the halogen oven, place the low rack inside the oven and replace the lid. Preheat the oven to 190°C.

2   Finely grate the rind from the lime, cut in half and squeeze out the juice. Cut the dates in half lengthways and halve the cherries.

3   Sprinkle 25g/1 oz of the sugar over the base of the dish and arrange the dates and cherries on top.

4   Sift the flour and mixed spice into a large bowl. Break the eggs into the flour and add the remaining sugar, butter, milk, lime juice and rind.

5   With a wooden spoon beat until well mixed, light and fluffy. Spoon the mixture over the dates and cherries and smooth the surface.

6   Put into the hot oven and cook for 20–30 minutes until risen and firm to the touch. Loosen the edges of the sponge and carefully turn out onto a plate. Remove the paper lining and serve immediately.

PEAR TART

A version of the well known French apple tart – Tarte Tatin. A fantastic dessert with few ingredients and little effort. Make individual tarts if you prefer and vary the fruit depending on the season. You will need a base-lined shallow 20cm/8 inch ovenproof dish or cake tin which fits in your oven.

SERVES 4–6	375g packet ready-rolled flaky pastry
	3 pears
	25g/1 oz soft butter
	4 tbsp light muscovado sugar

1   Remove the lid from the halogen oven, place the low rack inside the oven and replace the lid. Preheat the oven to 190°C.

2   Unroll the pastry and cut out a circle to fit just inside the dish.

3   Quarter the pears, remove and discard the cores and stalks and thickly slice.

4   Spread the butter over the bottom of the dish and sprinkle over the sugar. Arrange the pear slices in a pattern over the base and cover with the pastry disc.

5   Put into the hot oven and cook for 18 25 minutes until the pastry is cooked and the fruit soft. Leave in the dish for a few minutes and turn out onto a flat plate. Carefully remove the lining paper.

Plum and Ricotta Tart

Ricotta is a fresh cheese with a slightly sweet flavour. Smoother than cottage cheese it is used in many Italian desserts. Other fruits to use with this recipe are ripe peaches, nectarines or apricots. You will need an ovenproof 20cm/8 inch flan dish which fits in your oven.

SERVES 4–6

375g packet of ready-rolled shortcrust pastry
8 ripe plums
2 medium eggs
250g carton ricotta cheese

1 tsp vanilla extract
2 tbsp soft brown sugar
1–2 tbsp clear honey

1 Remove the lid from the halogen oven, place the low rack inside the oven and replace the lid. Preheat the oven to 180°C.

2 Unroll the pastry, and roll out until very thin. Loosely lay it over the flan dish. Press the pastry into the base and sides, trim away the excess and neaten the edges. Prick the base with a fork.

3 Put into the hot oven and cook for 6–8 minutes to 'set' the pastry. Leave to cool a little.

4 Cut the plums in half and remove the stones.

5 Lightly beat the eggs in a mixing bowl. Add the ricotta, vanilla extract and sugar and, using a whisk, beat until smooth.

6 Spoon the mixture into the flan case. Arrange the plum halves, cut side uppermost over the filling and drizzle over some of the honey.

7 Put into the hot oven and cook for 20–25 minutes until the pastry is cooked and the filling has set.

Spiced Bananas and Grapes

A quick and easy dish to prepare and cook. Serve with hot waffles and a scoop of vanilla ice cream. You will need an ovenproof dish which fits in your oven.

SERVES 4	
1 lime	4 tbsp clear honey
175g/6 oz seedless green grapes	2 tbsp light brown sugar
4 large bananas	½ tsp ground cinnamon
150ml/¼ pint unsweetened apple juice	½ tsp ground ginger

1   Remove the lid from the halogen oven, place the low rack inside the oven and replace the lid. Preheat the oven to 200°C.

2   Finely grate the rind from the lime, cut in half and squeeze out the juice. Halve the grapes, peel the bananas and cut into thick slices.

3   Pour the apple juice into the dish and stir in the lime juice and rind, honey, sugar, cinnamon and ginger.

4   Add the grapes and banana slices and mix until thoroughly coated – prevents the banana from discolouring.

5   Put into the hot oven and cook for 5 minutes, stir the fruit and sauce then cook for a further 5–10 minutes until the banana and grapes have softened and browned a little.

POACHED FRUITS WITH CRUNCHY SEEDS

Serve the fruits and topping with low-fat yogurt. Make larger quantities of the 'seedy' topping and keep in the freezer. You will need an ovenproof dish and a baking tray which fit in your oven.

SERVES 4–6

2 eating apples
1 orange
1 pomegranate
8 apricots
300ml/½ pint unsweetened apricot juice
3 tbsp soft brown sugar

Topping
3 tbsp jumbo oats
2 tbsp sunflower oil
1 tbsp plain flour
1 tbsp caster sugar
1 tbsp pumpkin seeds
1 tbsp sunflower seeds

1. Remove the lid from the halogen oven, place the low rack inside the oven and replace the lid. Preheat the oven to 190°C.

2. Quarter the apples, remove and discard the cores, and cut into wedges. Finely grate the rind from the orange, cut in half and squeeze out the juice. Cut the pomegranate in half and scoop out the seeds. Halve the apricots and remove the stones.

3. Pour the apricot juice into the dish and stir in the sugar and all the fruits.

4. Put into the hot oven and cook for 15–20 minutes or until the fruits are soft.

5. Put all of the topping ingredients into a mixing bowl and stir together with a fork.

6. Tip the crumbly seed mix onto the baking tray. Lift off the oven lid and put the high rack into the oven. Put the seed mix into the oven on the high rack and cook for 5–10 minutes until slightly 'toasted'.

7. Spoon the fruits into serving bowls and sprinkle over some of the topping.

Papaya and Figs in Red Wine

This recipe is suitable for all sorts of fruits although papaya and figs seem exotic. Papaya tastes like a cross between peaches and melon. If you can bring yourself to use it in a dessert, a little chilli will add warmth to the dish. You will need a shallow ovenproof dish which fits in your oven.

SERVES 4

1 large ripe papaya
6 figs
1–2 sprigs of mint
A small piece of fresh red chilli, optional
  (see page 19)

300ml/½ pint red wine or red grape juice
2 tbsp maple syrup or clear honey

1 Remove the lid from the halogen oven, place the high rack inside the oven and replace the lid. Preheat the oven to 180°C.

2 Peel the papaya, cut in half and scoop out the seeds and discard. Slice the figs in half through the stalks. Pull the leaves off the sprigs of mint; you'll need 8. If using, halve the chilli, remove and discard the seeds and finely chop.

3 Put the fruits (with a little chilli if using) and mint leaves into the dish, making sure the leaves are under the fruits – the fan may cause them to move.

4 Pour over the wine or grape juice and drizzle over the maple syrup or honey.

5 Put into the hot oven and cook for 15–20 minutes until the fruits are soft, stirring once if necessary.

Sweet Orange and Chocolate Pizza

Pizza fans will love this pud made with store-cupboard ingredients. In place of pizza bases, use your favourite flatbreads or nan breads. I've cooked the pizza on a baking sheet but it could be put directly onto the rack. Serve with Greek yogurt or ice cream. You will need a baking sheet which fits in your oven.

SERVES 3–4

285g can mandarin orange segments
12 mini marshmallows
One 20–23cm/8–9 inch ready-made pizza base
6 tbsp chocolate spread, with or without nuts
2 tbsp desiccated coconut

1 Remove the lid from the halogen oven, place the high rack inside the oven and replace the lid. Preheat the oven to 180°C.

2 Drain the can of mandarin orange segments. Cut each marshmallow in half.

3 Put the pizza base onto the baking sheet, or directly onto the rack. Swirl the chocolate spread on top, taking it almost to the edge – use a little more or less as you prefer.

4 Arrange the orange segments over the top, scatter over the marshmallow pieces and sprinkle over the coconut.

5 Put into the hot oven and cook for about 4–6 minutes until the pizza is piping hot and the topping has 'toasted' (be careful not to overcook the coconut). Cut into wedges and serve immediately.

Rose Apricots and Plums

A very elegant dessert, yet so easy to make. The flavours and tastes of apricots and plums, almond paste and rose water are a delight. Serve with small sweet crisp biscuits or meringues, pouring cream, yogurt or sorbet. You will need a wide shallow ovenproof dish which fits in your oven.

SERVES 4

500g/1 lb 2 oz ripe apricots and plums
250g/9 oz almond paste
25g/1 oz caster sugar
Rose water, to taste

1   Remove the lid from the halogen oven, place the low rack inside the oven and replace the lid. Preheat the oven to 190°C.

2   Cut the apricots and plums in half and remove the stones.

3   Arrange them in the dish in a single layer, cut side uppermost.

4   Tear off pieces of almond paste, roughly roll into balls and put on top of each piece of fruit.

5   Pour 150ml/¼ pint hot water around the fruits and sprinkle over the sugar.

6   Cover tightly with a lid or foil. Put into the hot oven and cook for 20–30 minutes until the fruits are just tender. Stir in a little rose water to taste and leave to cool.

CHOCOLATE AND RASPBERRY DELIGHT

A dense, dark rich chocolate cake or torte made with very little flour. You will need a greased base-lined 18cm/7 inch cake tin which fits in your oven.

SERVES 4–6		
	2 medium eggs	2 tbsp milk
	115g/4 oz caster sugar	25g/1 oz plain flour
	25g/1 oz butter, melted	1 tbsp cocoa powder
	125g/4½ oz dark chocolate with about 70% cocoa solids, melted	2 tbsp icing sugar
		350g/12 oz raspberries

1 Remove the lid from the halogen oven, place the low rack inside the oven and replace the lid. Preheat the oven to 180°C.

2 Separate the eggs, putting the yolks into a mixing bowl and the whites into a grease-free bowl.

3 Pour the sugar over the egg yolks and whisk until light and fluffy. Stir in the butter, chocolate and the milk.

4 Sieve the flour and cocoa into the bowl and gently stir until mixed.

5 Whisk the egg whites until like soft peaks and with a metal spoon carefully fold into the chocolate mixture. Spoon the mixture into the cake tin.

6 Put into the hot oven and cook for 20–25 minutes until cooked through. Serve warm or cold.

7 Sieve the icing sugar into a small bowl and then press half of the raspberries through the sieve. Mix to a smooth purée.

8 Serve slices of the chocolate cake dusted with icing sugar, drizzled with purée and top each portion with whole raspberries.

MANGO, APPLE AND PEANUT CRUMBLE

Mangoes have a lovely perfume and taste both sweet and tart, an ideal partner for crisp dessert apples. Peanuts add crunch to the crumble topping but make sure they are unsalted. You will need a shallow ovenproof dish about 850ml/1½ pint capacity which fits in your oven.

SERVES 4

1 large mango
3 dessert apples
2 tbsp light brown sugar

Topping
175g/6 oz plain flour
85g/3 oz unsalted butter
85g/3 oz light brown sugar
3 tbsp chopped unsalted peanuts

1   Remove the lid from the halogen oven, place the low rack inside the oven and replace the lid. Preheat the oven to 180°C.

2   Peel the mango and cut the flesh away from the stone in chunky pieces. Quarter the apples, remove and discard the cores, and cut into thick wedges.

3   Put the fruit into the dish, sprinkle over the sugar and pour over 3 tbsp cold water.

4   For the topping, tip the flour into a bowl. Cut the butter into small pieces and add to the flour. Using your fingertips, rub the butter into the mix until it resembles coarse crumbs. Stir in the sugar and peanuts.

5   Sprinkle the topping thickly and evenly over the fruit, pressing down lightly.

6   Put into the hot oven and cook for 25–35 minutes until cooked and golden.

Gooseberry and Sultana Pudding

Gooseberries give a pleasant sharpness to this layered pudding. Serve with custard or reduced fat crème fraîche. You will need a greased and base-lined 20cm/8 inch ovenproof dish which fits in your oven.

SERVES 4–6

500g/1 lb 2 oz gooseberries, fresh or frozen
175g/6 oz wholemeal flour
115g/4 oz butter
55g/2 oz caster sugar
60g/2¼ oz desiccated coconut

55g/2 oz soft brown sugar
½ tsp ground ginger
85g/3 oz sultanas

1 Remove the lid from the halogen oven, place the low rack inside the oven and replace the lid. Preheat the oven to 190°C.

2 Top and tail fresh gooseberries if using. Tip the flour into a mixing bowl. Cut the butter into small cubes and add to the flour. Using your fingertips, rub the butter into the flour until the mixture resembles fine crumbs and mix in the caster sugar.

3 In a small bowl mix together the coconut, brown sugar and ginger.

4 Sprinkle a little of the coconut mixture over the base of the dish and cover with half of the gooseberries. Scatter over the sultanas, the remaining coconut mix and gooseberries.

5 Spoon the crumb mixture evenly over the fruit and gently press down.

6 Put into the hot oven and cook for about 40–55 minutes until piping hot and cooked through. Leave in the tin for 5 minutes, turn onto a flat plate and remove the lining paper.

STICKY ROASTED PINEAPPLE AND ORANGES WITH PANCAKES

Roasted fruits become slightly caramelised on the edges. Serve them with a little single cream or yogurt. Alternatively, spoon the fruits onto toasted slices of brioche bread or hot waffles. You will need foil and a wide ovenproof dish or roasting tin which fits in your oven.

SERVES 4–6	4–6 ready-made pancakes	Thick Greek yogurt, to serve
	1 medium pineapple	50g/1¾ oz chopped nuts, such as pistachios,
	2 small oranges	almonds, hazelnuts
	1 tbsp oil	
	3 tbsp clear honey or golden syrup	

1   Remove the lid from the halogen oven, place the low and high rack inside the oven and replace the lid. Preheat the oven to 180°C.

2   Stack the pancakes and wrap in a large piece of foil, keeping them flat. Cut the top and base off the pineapple and cut away the thick rind. Cut lengthways into four pieces, remove the core if hard, and thickly slice each quarter. Peel the oranges, removing all the skin and white pith. With a small sharp knife remove the segments.

3   Pour the oil, honey (or syrup), and 2 tbsp cold water into the cooking dish and mix thoroughly. Add the prepared fruit and gently turn the pieces over in the syrup until coated.

4   Arrange the fruits in a single layer. Put into the hot oven and cook for 10 minutes.

5   Remove the lid from the oven, take out the dish of fruits and the high rack and put onto a heatproof surface. Place the foil parcel of pancakes on the low rack and return the high rack and fruits to the oven. Close the lid and cook for 5 minutes or until the fruits are just cooked and lightly browned at the edges.

6   Spoon some of the fruits onto the heated pancakes, fold or roll the pancake over the filling and serve with a spoonful of yogurt sprinkled with the chopped nuts.

Hot Cinnamon Pears with Butterscotch Sauce

You could serve the pears and syrup on thick slices of fruit brioche and spoon over the sauce. Put the slices of brioche on the high shelf to toast for a few minutes. You will need a bowl for the sauce and a shallow ovenproof dish which fits in your oven.

SERVES 4

Butterscotch sauce
55g/2 oz butter
55g/2 oz soft brown sugar
4 tbsp golden syrup
1 tsp lemon juice
8 tbsp double cream

4 pears
5cm/2 inch cinnamon stick
2 star anise
300ml/½ pint sweet white wine or white grape juice
3 tbsp caster sugar

1   Remove the lid from the halogen oven, place the low rack inside the oven and replace the lid. (You will also need the high rack.) Preheat the halogen oven to 200°C.

2   Put the butter, sugar, golden syrup, lemon juice and cream into a bowl. Cover and put into the hot oven for 10 minutes.

3   Peel and quarter the pears, remove and discard the cores and stalks.

4   Put the pears, cinnamon stick and star anise into the dish. Pour over the wine or grape juice, stir in the caster sugar and cover the dish.

5   Remove the lid from the oven and lift out the bowl of sauce, stir thoroughly, cover and put back into the oven if it is not piping hot, but don't let it burn.

6   Put the high rack in place and put the dish of pears on top. Replace the lid and cook for 12–15 minutes until the pears are cooked through – this will depend on the ripeness of the pears.

7   Stir the sauce until smooth and serve spooned over the pears and syrup.

CHOCOLATE, ORANGE AND HAZELNUT CREAMS

A velvety dessert hides the surprise of warm orange segments beneath. You will need a baking tray which fits in your oven and four heatproof ramekin dishes.

SERVES 4	2 small oranges	3 tbsp double cream
	200g/7 oz dark chocolate	100g/3½ oz chopped hazelnuts
	200g/7 oz mascarpone cheese	

1   Remove the lid from the halogen oven, place the low rack inside the oven and replace the lid. Preheat the halogen oven to 200°C.

2   Finely grate the rind from part of one orange – you need 1 tsp rind. Peel the oranges, removing all the skin and white pith. With a small sharp knife, remove the segments and cut each in half. Grate the chocolate.

3   Spoon the mascarpone cheese into a bowl and stir in the orange rind, cream, grated chocolate and half of the chopped hazelnuts.

4   Put a few orange pieces into each ramekin dish. Spoon over some of the chocolate mixture and smooth the surface. Sprinkle the reserved nuts over the top.

5   Put the ramekins on to the baking tray and put into the hot oven. Cook for 12–18 minutes until piping hot – cover with foil if the surface begins to brown too much.

Apple and Ginger Pancakes

Ready-made pancakes are a useful standby. Serve with yogurt or ice cream. You will need a large buttered shallow ovenproof dish (to hold the pancakes in a single layer) which fits in your oven.

SERVES 4–6

25g/1 oz crystallised ginger, about 2 pieces
140g/5 oz cream cheese
150ml/¼ pint apple purée
1 tsp ground ginger

100g/3½ oz sultanas
4–6 ready-made pancakes
2 tbsp melted butter

1   Remove the lid from the halogen oven, place the high rack inside the oven and replace the lid. Preheat the halogen oven to 180°C.

2   Finely chop the crystallised ginger.

3   Put the cream cheese and apple purée into a bowl and mix in the ground ginger. Stir in the sultanas and chopped ginger.

4   Spread each pancake with some of the apple mixture.

5   Roll the pancakes over the filling and put in a single layer in the dish. Brush with the melted butter and cover with foil.

6   Put the dish into the hot oven and cook for 6–8 minutes until piping hot.

HOT APRICOT TRIFLE

It seems a strange concept but all the elements of a trifle are here. You will need a buttered ovenproof dish which fits in your oven and which holds four slices of cake in a single layer.

SERVES 4	8 apricots	300ml/½ pint prepared custard
	4 slices Madeira cake, or any plain cake	55g/2 oz soft brown sugar
	Apricot conserve, to spread	55g/2 oz soft butter
	2 tbsp amaretto liqueur (optional)	Whipped cream, to serve
	150ml/¼ pint apricot juice	

1 Remove the lid from the halogen oven, place the low rack inside the oven and replace the lid. Preheat the halogen oven to 180°C.

2 Halve the apricots, remove the stones and cut each into quarters.

3 Thickly spread the cake slices with apricot conserve. Spoon the liqueur, if using, into the apricot juice and drizzle evenly over the cake slices

4 Pour over the custard and arrange the apricot quarters on top. Sprinkle over the sugar and dot the butter over the surface.

5 Put the dish into the hot oven and cook 15–20 minutes until hot and the apricots have softened. Cover with foil if it is browning too much. Serve with whipped cream.

Blueberry and Strawberry Brioche Pudding

A variation on 'bread and butter pudding'. Brioche bread gives a richness to the pudding; you could try using thin slices of white sourdough bread. Serve with a fruit sauce. You will need a buttered shallow dish which fits in your oven.

SERVES 4–6

A handful of strawberries
8 slices plain brioche bread, about 250g/9 oz
3 large eggs
175g/6 oz mascarpone cheese
2 tbsp maple syrup or caster sugar

600ml/1 pint milk
A handful of blueberries
1 tbsp grated lemon rind
Icing sugar, to dust

1   Remove the lid from the halogen oven, place the low rack inside the oven and replace the lid. Preheat the oven to 170°C.

2   Twist the stalks off the strawberries and thickly slice. Cut the bread into fingers, or squares – the size doesn't really matter.

3   Break the eggs into a mixing bowl and add the mascarpone cheese, maple syrup or caster sugar. Slowly stir in the milk and mix until smooth.

4   Arrange half the bread pieces in the bottom of the dish. Scatter the blueberries, strawberry slices and lemon rind evenly over the layer of bread. Cover with the remaining bread pieces.

5   Slowly pour the egg mixture over the bread. Leave to stand for 30 minutes.

6   Put the dish into the hot oven and bake for 30–40 minutes until firm and cooked through. Dust with icing sugar before serving.

ROASTED PINEAPPLE WEDGES

Little effort is needed to produce this quick yet impressive dessert. You will need a large shallow ovenproof dish which fits in your oven.

SERVES 4–6

1 ripe pineapple
1 lime
4 tbsp light brown sugar
3 tbsp rum
Pinch ground black pepper

1   Remove the lid from the halogen oven, place the high rack inside the oven and replace the lid. Preheat the halogen oven to 200°C.

2   Cut the top and base off the pineapple. Slice lengthways into four or six pieces depending on the size, and cut away the core. Finely grate the rind from the lime to give 2 tsp. Cut in half and squeeze the juice.

3   In a small bowl mix together the lime rind and juice, sugar, rum, and black pepper.

4   Brush the rum mixture over the cut sides of the pineapple wedges. Arrange in a single layer in the dish.

5   Put the dish into the hot oven and cook for 3–5 minutes until the pineapple is beginning to brown, but don't let it burn. Remove the lid from the oven and lift out the dish. Replace the lid and set the timer for 10 minutes. Turn the pineapple wedges over and brush with any remaining rum mixture. Return to the oven and cook for 2–3 minutes until browned. Serve immediately.

CRÈME BRÛLÉE

My version of this well-known dessert. It is also delicious made using different fruits or flavoured with a tablespoon of strong coffee or melted dark chocolate. You will need a baking tray which fits in your oven and four heatproof ramekin dishes.

SERVES 4

200g/7 oz blueberries, thawed if frozen
150ml/¼ pint crème fraîche
150ml/¼ pint prepared custard
2 tsp clear honey
4 tbsp brown sugar

1   Remove the lid from the halogen oven, place the high rack inside the oven and replace the lid. Preheat the halogen oven to 200°C

2   Divide the blueberries between the ramekin dishes. Put them onto the baking tray and put into the hot oven. Cook for 3–4 minutes until the blueberries are just beginning to soften and burst. Remove from the oven.

3   Spoon the crème fraîche into a bowl and stir in the custard and honey. Spoon some of the mixture into each ramekin dish and smooth the surface. Sprinkle the sugar over the top.

4   Put the ramekins on the baking tray and into the hot oven. Turn the heat to 220–250°C. Cook for 10–15 minutes until the sugar melts and caramelises – cover with foil if the surface begins to brown too much. Chill before serving.

MIXED BERRY BAKED CHEESECAKE

A pastry case with a vanilla flavoured curd cheese, soured cream and fruit filling. Serve cold with fruit purée, or just on its own. Omit the fruits and serve a plain vanilla cheesecake with poached or fresh fruits. You will need an ovenproof 20cm/8 inch deep flan tin or dish which fits in your oven.

SERVES 4–6

175g/6 oz mixed berries, such as raspberries, blueberries, blackberries, fresh or frozen
375g packet ready-rolled shortcrust pastry
2 medium eggs
225g/8 oz curd cheese

55g/2 oz soft brown sugar
150ml/5½ fl oz soured cream
½ tsp vanilla extract
Icing sugar, to sift

1   Remove the lid from the halogen oven, place the low rack inside the oven and replace the lid. Preheat the oven to 180°C.

2   If using fresh fruits remove any leaves or stalks; if using frozen ones dry on kitchen paper.

3   Unroll the pastry and roll out until very thin. Loosely lay it over the flan tin or dish. Press the pastry into the base and sides, trim away the excess and neaten the edges. Prick the base with a fork.

4   Put into the hot oven and cook for 6–10 minutes, or until the pastry is cooked. Leave to cool a little.

5   Separate the eggs, putting the yolks into a mixing bowl and the whites into a grease-free bowl.

6   To the egg yolks, add the curd cheese, sugar, soured cream and vanilla. Mix until smooth and stir in the berries.

7   Whisk the egg whites until like soft peaks and with a metal spoon carefully fold into the berry mixture. Spoon into the flan case and smooth the top.

8   Put into the hot oven and cook for 20–30 minutes or until the pastry is cooked and the filling has set. Cool and dust with icing sugar.

6. TEMPTING BAKES

Who can resist the enticing smells of home baking from the oven? You can't help thinking about the taste to come. Sink your teeth into a piping hot scone or cookie; savour the intense aroma as you bite into a slice of freshly baked bread; or enjoy with heightened satisfaction a slice of cake which you have artfully created. There is really nothing like it. And now with your halogen oven you can do all this, and experience the same eagerness and pleasure, with the baking time reduced.

The recipes in this section show by their range just what you can achieve and what you can look forward to. Just try a date and walnut scone (page 176), a piece of cornbread (page 174), or a slice of fruit cake (page 181).

CHOC-CHIP AND ALMOND COOKIES

Crisp on the outside and slightly soft in the middle, these tempting cookies should be stored in an airtight tin. You will need a greased baking tray which fits in your oven.

MAKES about 10

85g/3 oz self-raising flour
55g/2 oz light brown caster sugar
55g/2 oz soft butter
Few drops vanilla extract

1 small egg
40g/1½ oz plain or milk chocolate chips
40g/1½ oz chopped almonds

1   Remove the lid from the halogen oven, place the high rack inside the oven and replace the lid. Preheat the oven to 160°C.

2   Sift the flour into a mixing bowl and stir in the sugar, butter, vanilla extract and egg. Mix until smooth and stir in the chocolate chips and almonds.

3   Put teaspoons of the mixture onto the greased baking tray, leaving space for them to spread.

4   Put into the hot oven and cook for 10–12 minutes or until firm and light golden brown. (Bake in batches if necessary.) Cool on a wire rack.

CINNAMON SHORTBREAD WEDGES

Shortbread can be dusted with a little icing sugar or dipped into melted chocolate. Add a tablespoon of finely chopped toasted hazelnuts or a little lemon rind to the mix. You will need a greased baking tray which fits in your oven.

MAKES 8 wedges

115g/4 oz plain flour
¼ tsp ground cinnamon
55g/2 oz ground rice
55g/2 oz caster sugar

55g/2 oz butter
Caster sugar, to sprinkle

1 Remove the lid from the halogen oven, place the low rack inside the oven and replace the lid. Preheat the oven to 180°C.

2 Sift the flour and ground cinnamon into a large bowl and stir in the ground rice and sugar.

3 Cut the butter into small cubes and add to the bowl. Using your fingertips, rub the butter into the flour mixture until the mixture resembles fine crumbs. Gently knead to form a soft smooth dough.

4 Roll or press the dough into a large round shape about 1cm/½ inch thick and put onto the baking tray. Pinch the edges to decorate, prick all over with a fork and score into eight portions.

5 Put into the hot oven and cook for 25–35 minutes or until pale golden, firm and cooked through. Cut into wedges while still warm, sprinkle over a little sugar and cool on a wire rack.

Pecan and Blueberry Muffins

Muffins are so quick and easy to make – the cake mixture doesn't even have to be smooth, just left slightly lumpy. In place of dried blueberries I sometimes use fresh or frozen berries, the texture will be a little softer. Replace the blueberries with your favourite ready-to-eat dried fruits and nuts such as apricot and almonds or cherries and walnuts. You will need a greased muffin tin which fits in your oven.

MAKES 10–12	300g/10½ oz self-raising flour	250ml/9 fl oz milk
	1 tsp baking powder	½ tsp vanilla extract
	2 medium eggs	60g/2¼ oz ready-to-eat dried blueberries
	50g/1¾ oz golden caster sugar	50g/1¾ oz chopped pecan nuts
	4 tbsp sunflower oil	Icing sugar, to sift

1 Remove the lid from the halogen oven, place the low rack inside the oven and replace the lid. Preheat the oven to 190°C.

2 Sift the flour and baking powder into a large bowl. Break the eggs into the flour and add the sugar, oil, milk, vanilla extract, blueberries and pecan nuts.

3 With a wooden spoon, lightly beat the ingredients together until they are just mixed (don't worry if the mixture is still a little lumpy – it is important not to over mix). Spoon into the muffin tins. (Bake in batches if necessary.)

4 Put into the hot oven and cook for 12–15 minutes until risen and firm to the touch. Cool on a wire rack.

5 When cold, sift a little icing sugar on top of each muffin.

ORANGE CUP-CAKES TOPPED WITH FLUFFY CREAM CHEESE ICING

Cup-cakes are always a traditional favourite. Add a touch of glamour with a swirl of orange icing and your own creative decoration. You will need a bun tin which fits in your oven.

MAKES about 15–18

1 orange
140g/5 oz self-raising flour
2 medium eggs
115g/4 oz golden caster sugar
115g/4 oz soft butter

Orange icing
225g/8 oz icing sugar
85g/3 oz low-fat cream cheese
Small sweets, coloured sugar strands, crystallised pieces of orange or sugared flowers, for decoration

1   Remove the lid from the halogen oven, place the low rack inside the oven and replace the lid. Preheat the oven to 190°C.

2   Finely grate the rind from the orange, cut in half and squeeze the juice from the whole orange.

3   Sift the flour into a large bowl. Break the eggs into the flour and add the sugar, butter and half of the grated orange rind.

4   With a wooden spoon or mixer, lightly beat the ingredients together until thoroughly mixed, light and fluffy. Spoon into the bun tin (bake in 2–3 batches if necessary).

5   Put into the hot oven and cook for 12–15 minutes until risen, firm to the touch and cooked through. Cool on a wire rack.

6   Sift the icing sugar into a bowl and stir in the cream cheese, the remaining grated orange rind and 1 tbsp orange juice. Mix until light and fluffy, adding more juice if necessary to give a spreadable consistency.

7   Swirl some of the icing on top of each cake and decorate as you wish.

MACAROON BARS

These bars are equally delicious when made with shortcrust or flaky pastry. Use your favourite flavoured conserve or jam. You will need a greased shallow baking tin about 20cm/8 inches square which fits in your oven.

MAKES 10–12 bars

2 medium eggs
60g/2¼ oz self-raising flour
50g/1¾ oz ground almonds
100g/3½ oz caster sugar
100g/3½ oz soft butter

5 sheets of filo pastry
2 tsp sunflower oil
3 tbsp raspberry conserve or jam
50g/1¾ oz flaked almonds

1　Remove the lid from the halogen oven, place the low rack inside the oven and replace the lid. Preheat the oven to 190°C.

2　Separate the eggs by putting the yolks into a mixing bowl and the whites into a grease-free bowl.

3　Sift the flour over the egg yolks and add the ground almonds, sugar and butter. Mix with a wooden spoon until light and fluffy.

4　Whisk the egg whites until like soft peaks and with a metal spoon carefully fold into the almond mixture.

5　Unroll the filo pastry, keeping it covered with clear film until needed. Working quickly, brush a pastry sheet with a little oil and line the tin, leaving the excess hanging over the sides. Repeat with another four sheets of pastry, placing them at alternate angles. Trim off any excess pastry.

6　Spread the conserve or jam over the pastry base and spoon over the almond mixture. Scatter the flaked almonds over the surface.

7　Put into the hot oven and cook for 20–25 minutes until cooked through and golden. Leave in the tin for 10 minutes to cool slightly before cutting into bars. Cool on a wire rack.

Apricot and Sesame Seed Flapjack

A sweet treat at any time of year. Replace the apricots with sultanas, dates, walnuts or almonds. You will need a greased shallow baking tin about 18cm/7 inches square which fits in your oven.

MAKES about 16–18 pieces

6 ready-to-eat dried apricots
55g/2 oz golden caster sugar
55g/2 oz soft butter

2 tbsp golden syrup
100g/3½ rolled oats
3 tbsp sesame seeds

1 Remove the lid from the halogen oven, place the low rack inside the oven and replace the lid. Preheat the oven to 170°C.

2 Coarsely chop the apricots.

3 Put the sugar, butter and syrup into a heatproof bowl. Carefully put into the oven and leave for seconds until the butter has melted (watching all the time).

4 Remove from the oven, place on a heatproof surface and cool a little before stirring in the oats, apricots and sesame seeds.

5 Press into the prepared tin. Put into the hot oven and cook for 15 minutes or until firm and cooked through.

6 Cut into squares, fingers or wedges whilst warm and cool on a wire rack.

CORNBREAD

A quick American bread made without yeast and using cornmeal in place of some flour. Buttermilk gives a tangy flavour, but if it isn't available add a few drops of lemon juice to fresh milk. You will need a greased and base-lined square cake tin which fits in your oven.

SERVES 4–6

125g/4½ oz cornmeal
125g/4½ oz plain flour
1 tsp baking powder
½ tsp bicarbonate of soda

1 tsp salt
2 medium eggs
85g/3 oz butter, melted
200ml/7 fl oz buttermilk, plus extra if needed

1   Remove the lid from the halogen oven, place the low rack inside the oven and replace the lid. Preheat the oven to 200°C.

2   Tip the cornmeal into a large mixing bowl and sift in the flour, baking powder, bicarbonate of soda and salt. Break the eggs into the bowl and pour in the melted butter.

3   With a wooden spoon, stir the buttermilk into the cornmeal mixture and mix to a smooth soft consistency. Add a little extra buttermilk if needed.

4   Spoon into the prepared tin and cook in the hot oven for 20 minutes until firm and golden brown. Serve warm.

ICED LEMON AND LIME CUP-CAKES

I often make these using half white and half wholemeal flour for a slightly denser cake. You will need a bun tin lined with paper cake cases which fits in your oven.

MAKES	1 lemon	Lemon and Lime Icing
about 15 10	1 lime	250g/9 oz icing sugar
	140g/5 oz self-raising flour	Few drops yellow food colouring
	2 medium eggs	Few drops green food colouring
	115g/4 oz caster sugar	
	115g/4 oz soft butter	

1   Remove the lid from the halogen oven, place the low rack inside the oven and replace the lid. Preheat the halogen oven to 190°C.

2   Finely grate the rind from the lemon to give 1 tsp, cut the lemon in half and squeeze the juice from both halves. Strain the juice into a cup. Finely grate the rind from the lime to give 1 tsp, cut the lime in half and squeeze the juice from both halves. Strain the juice into another cup.

3   Sift the flour into a large bowl. Break the eggs into the flour and add the sugar, butter and the grated lemon and lime rind.

4   With a wooden spoon or mixer, lightly beat the ingredients together until thoroughly mixed, light and fluffy. Spoon into the paper cases (bake in 2–3 batches if necessary).

5   Put into the hot oven and cook for 12–15 minutes until risen, firm to the touch and cooked through. Cool on a wire tray.

6   Sift half of the icing sugar into one bowl and the remainder into a second bowl. Add a drop or two of yellow colouring to one bowl, and with a wooden spoon mix in enough lemon juice to give a smooth almost flowing icing. Add a little cold water if necessary. Repeat with the second bowl of icing sugar, this time using the green colouring and lime juice.

7   Spread or spoon a little lemon icing over half of each cake and repeat with the lime icing over the other half. With a skewer or prongs of a fork, zigzag or swirl the icing together along the join. Leave to set.

DATE AND WALNUT SCONES

Deluxe scones, delicious served warm. Cherry and almond, or cranberry and hazelnut are also favourite variations. Or, replace half of the flour with wholemeal self-raising flour. You will need a baking tray dusted with flour which fits in your oven.

MAKES 8–10

50g/1¾ oz ready-to-eat dried dates
50g/1¾ oz walnut pieces
1 medium egg
225g/8 oz self-raising flour, plus extra for rolling
1 tsp baking powder

½ tsp ground mixed spice
50g/1¾ oz butter
50g/1¾ oz golden caster sugar
About 5 tbsp milk, plus extra for brushing

1   Remove the lid from the halogen oven, place the high rack inside the oven and replace the lid. Preheat the oven to 200°C.

2   Coarsely chop the dates and walnuts. In a small bowl lightly beat the egg.

3   Into a large bowl, sift the flour, baking powder and mixed spice. Cut the butter into small cubes and add to the flour. Using your fingertips, rub the butter into the flour until the mixture resembles fine crumbs and mix in the sugar, dates and walnuts.

4   Using a round-bladed table knife, mix to a soft dough with the egg and some of the milk.

5   Turn onto a lightly floured surface and knead gently until smooth. Roll or pat the dough into a rough round shape about 1cm/½ inch thick. Cut into discs with a 6cm/2½ inch cutter or cut into squares with a sharp knife.

6   Lift the scones onto the prepared tray and brush the tops with a little milk. Put into the hot oven and cook for 10–12 minutes or until well risen, golden brown and cooked through. (Bake in batches if necessary.) Cool on a wire rack.

STICKY RAISIN AND LEMON GINGERBREAD

Gingerbread improves with keeping for a day or two. Replace the raisins with sultanas and scatter flaked almonds over the surface. For a more intense flavour, replace the golden syrup with molasses. You will need a greased and base-lined 18cm/7 inch deep cake tin (square or round) which fits in your oven.

SERVES 6–8

115g/4 oz butter
55g/2 oz soft brown sugar
140g/5 oz golden syrup
3 tbsp black treacle
250g/9 oz plain flour
3 tsp ground ginger

1 tsp bicarbonate of soda
150ml/¼ pint milk
1 medium egg
85g/3 oz raisins
2 tsp grated lemon rind

1 Remove the lid from the halogen oven, place the low rack inside the oven and replace the lid. Preheat the oven to 180°C.

2 Either put the butter, sugar, syrup and treacle into a saucepan and heat until just melted, then pour into a mixing bowl, or, put the ingredients into a large heatproof bowl. Carefully put into the oven and leave for seconds until just melted (watching all the time). Leave to cool.

3 Sift the flour, ginger and bicarbonate of soda into the cooled mixture. Stir in the milk, egg, raisins and lemon rind. Mix thoroughly and spoon into the prepared tin.

4 Put into the hot oven and cook for 45–55 minutes or until risen and firm, but look at the cake after 35 minutes in case it is ready. Cool on a wire rack and cut into slices or squares.

Lemon and Orange Drizzle Cake

A well-known traditional cake to which I've added ground almonds. Bite into a slice and taste the intense citrus flavours of the sweet glaze which is poured over the hot cake. You will need a greased and base-lined 18cm/7 inch deep cake tin (square or round) which fits in your oven.

SERVES 6–8		
	1 orange	60g/2¼ oz ground almonds
	1 lemon	125g/4½ oz golden caster sugar
	175g/6 oz self-raising flour	125g/4½ oz soft butter
	1 tsp baking powder	100g/3½ oz icing sugar
	2 medium eggs	

1   Remove the lid from the halogen oven, place the low rack inside the oven and replace the lid. Preheat the oven to 180°C.

2   Finely grate the rind from half the orange and half the lemon, cut both in half and squeeze the juice from the whole fruits (you will need about 6 tbsp). Mix the juices together in a small basin.

3   Sift the flour and baking powder into a large bowl. Break the eggs into the flour and add the ground almonds, sugar, butter, orange and lemon rinds and 3 tbsp fruit juice.

4   With a wooden spoon or mixer, lightly beat the ingredients together until thoroughly mixed, light and fluffy. Spoon into the prepared tin and level the surface.

5   Put into the hot oven and cook for 20–25 minutes until risen, firm to the touch and cooked through.

6   Whilst the cake is cooking, make the drizzle mixture. Sieve the icing sugar into a bowl, pour in the remaining 3 tbsp fruit juices and mix to a smooth paste.

7   Turn the cake onto a wire rack and whilst still hot use a fine skewer to make several holes in the top of the cake. Spoon the drizzle mixture over the top of the cake and leave to cool.

COFFEE CAKE WITH BUTTERSCOTCH CREAM

What a treat, very delicious and difficult to resist a second slice. For a simpler version, sandwich the cake with lemon curd and dust with a little icing sugar. You will need a greased and base-lined 18cm/7 inch deep round cake tin which fits in your oven.

SERVES 6–8

2 tsp instant coffee granules
2 large eggs
125g/4½ oz self-raising flour
1 tsp baking powder
125g/4½ oz soft butter

125g/4½ oz golden caster sugar
60g/2¼ oz brittle butterscotch or barley sugar sweets
150ml/¼ pint double cream

1 Remove the lid from the halogen oven, place the low rack inside the oven and replace the lid. Preheat the oven to 190°C.

2 Tip the coffee granules into a small bowl and dissolve in 1 tbsp boiling water and cool.

3 Break the eggs into a mixing bowl and sift in the flour and baking powder. Add the butter, sugar and cooled coffee. Mix until smooth and fluffy then spoon into the prepared tin.

4 Put into the hot oven and cook for 45–55 minutes or until risen and golden brown. Turn onto a wire rack.

5 Put the butterscotch or barley sugar sweets into a freezer bag and break into small pieces by tapping with a rolling pin. Pour the cream into a bowl and lightly whip. Stir the crushed butterscotch/barley sugar into the cream, reserving a few pieces for decoration.

6 Slice the cake in half horizontally through the middle. Put the bottom layer onto a plate and with a knife spread over half of the cream mixture. Cover with the second layer of cake, swirl the remaining cream mixture on top and scatter over the reserved butterscotch.

FRUIT CAKE

A semi-rich fruit cake which keeps well and can be frozen. Ring the changes with your own choice of fruits or nuts. You will need a greased and base-lined 20cm/8 inch deep round cake tin which fits in your oven.

SERVES 8–10

1 orange
225g/8 oz self-raising flour
1 tsp baking powder
1½ tsp ground mixed spice
2 medium eggs
140g/5 oz golden caster sugar

140g/5 oz soft butter
175g/6 oz mixed dried fruits, sultanas, raisins and currants
175g/6 oz ready-to-eat dried blueberries or cranberries
Approx 100ml/3½ fl oz milk

1   Remove the lid from the halogen oven, place the low rack inside the oven and replace the lid. Preheat the oven to 160°C.

2   Finely grate the rind from the orange, cut the orange in half and squeeze the juice.

3   Sift the flour, baking powder and mixed spice into a large bowl. Break the eggs into the flour and add the sugar, butter, dried fruits, blueberries or cranberries, milk, orange rind and juice.

4   With a wooden spoon or mixer thoroughly mix the ingredients together. Spoon into the prepared tin and level the surface.

5   Put into the hot oven and cook for ¾–1¼ hours until cooked through, and firm to the touch (a fine skewer when pushed into the centre of the cake should be clean when removed).

6   Leave in the tin for 5 minutes before turning onto a wire rack. Leave to cool.

WHOLEMEAL BREAD

A good basic everyday loaf. Cook the dough in a 450g/1 lb loaf tin or make into rolls. You will need a baking tray dusted with flour which fits in your oven.

SERVES 4–6

1 tsp clear honey
175g/6 oz strong wholemeal flour, plus extra for
  kneading
55g/2 oz strong white flour

½ tsp salt
¾ tsp fast-acting yeast
Milk, or beaten egg for brushing

1   Put the kettle on to boil, pour 150ml/¼ pint into a jug, stir in the honey and leave until tepid.

2   Mix the flour, salt and yeast in a large bowl. Pour over the tepid water and honey mixture and using your fingers gather the mix together to give a soft dough, adding more water if needed.

3   Turn the dough onto a lightly floured surface. Knead until smooth and shape into a ball.

4   Put onto the prepared tray, cover loosely with lightly oiled clear film and leave in a warm place until doubled in height, about 25–35 minutes. Brush with a little milk or beaten egg.

5   Meanwhile, remove the lid from the halogen oven, place the low rack inside the oven and replace the lid. Preheat the oven to 200°C.

6   Cook in the hot oven for 15–20 minutes until cooked and golden brown. The bread will sound hollow when tapped underneath.

FOCACCIA WITH SUN-DRIED TOMATOES, ROSEMARY AND GARLIC

An Italian flatbread eaten as a snack or served with soups and salads. I often replace the rosemary with sprigs of oregano and push slices of stoned black olives into the dough. You will need an oiled shallow baking tray or small roasting tin which fits in your oven.

SERVES 4–6

2 garlic cloves
A few rosemary sprigs
60g/2¼ oz ready-to-eat sun-dried tomatoes
250g/8 oz strong plain white flour, plus extra for kneading

½ tsp salt
½ tsp fast-acting yeast
3 tbsp olive oil, plus extra for drizzling
1 tsp coarse sea salt for sprinkling

1 Put the kettle on to boil, pour 150ml/¼ pint less 1 tbsp into a jug and leave until tepid. Peel and slice the garlic cloves. Pull the rosemary from the stalks and roughly chop, and finely chop the sun-dried tomatoes.

2 Mix the flour, salt and yeast in a large bowl. Pour over the tepid water and tomato pieces and 1 tbsp of the olive oil and using your fingers gather the mix together to give a soft dough, adding more water if needed.

3 Turn the dough onto a lightly floured surface. Knead until smooth and roll or push to roughly the shape of your tin.

4 Put the dough into the prepared tin and keep pressing and pushing to form an even layer (it will keep shrinking back, but persevere). Scatter garlic slices and rosemary over the dough and evenly drizzle over the remaining olive oil. Dimple the surface by pressing your fingertips into the dough. There is no need to cover, leave in a warm place until doubled in height, about 25–35 minutes.

5 Meanwhile, remove the lid from the halogen oven, place the low rack inside the oven and replace the lid. Preheat the oven to 200°C.

6 Cook in the hot oven for 15–20 minutes until cooked and golden brown. Remove from the oven and immediately drizzle over a little more oil and scatter over a little sea salt.

CHEESE AND HERB ROLLS

Serve these rolls whilst still warm and the cheese is soft. You will need a baking tray dusted with flour which fits in your oven.

MAKES 6

70g/2½ oz Cheddar cheese
250g/8 oz strong plain white flour, plus extra for
   kneading
½ tsp salt

½ tsp fast-acting yeast
2 tbsp chopped parsley, chives or coriander
Milk, or beaten egg for brushing

1   Put the kettle on to boil, pour 150ml/¼ pint into a jug and leave until tepid. Finely grate the cheese.

2   Mix the flour, salt and yeast in a large bowl. Mix in the grated cheese and chopped herbs.

3   Pour over the tepid water and using your fingers gather the mix together to give a soft dough, adding more water if needed.

4   Turn the dough onto a lightly floured surface and knead until smooth.

5   With a sharp knife cut the dough into six even sized pieces and shape each into a ball. Put onto the prepared tray, leaving space for them to rise. Cover loosely with lightly oiled clear film and leave in a warm place until doubled in height, about 20–30 minutes. Brush the rolls with a little milk or beaten egg.

6   Meanwhile, remove the lid from the halogen oven, place the low rack inside the oven and replace the lid. Preheat the oven to 200°C.

7   Cook in the hot oven for 12–15 minutes until cooked and golden brown. The bread will sound hollow when tapped underneath.

VIENNESE WHIRLS

Melt-in-the-mouth biscuits – dip them in melted chocolate and chopped nuts. It's easy to keep a good shape if the mixture is spooned or piped into cake cases. You will need a bun tin lined with paper cake cases which fits in your oven, or alternatively a flat buttered baking tray. Also, a piping bag and nozzle.

MAKES
about 15–18

125g/4½ oz plain flour
1 tbsp cornflour
2 tbsp drinking chocolate
25g/1 oz icing sugar

140g/5 oz soft butter
1 tsp grated orange rind
About 18 blanched almonds
Extra icing sugar for dusting

1   Remove the lid from the halogen oven, place the low rack inside the oven and replace the lid. Preheat the halogen oven to 200°C.

2   Sift the flour, cornflour and drinking chocolate into a small bowl. Sift the icing sugar into a mixing bowl.

3   Add the butter and orange rind to the icing sugar and mix with a wooden spoon or a mixer until light and fluffy. Gradually add the flour mixture and mix to a soft but firm piping consistency.

4   Spoon the mixture into a piping bag and pipe a ring of the mixture in the bottom of each cake case. Alternatively, put spoonfuls on the baking tray. Gently press an almond on top of each biscuit.

5   Put into the hot oven and cook for 10–15 minutes, until firm to the touch and cooked through. Cool on a wire tray and dust with a little sieved icing sugar.

DOUBLE CHOCOLATE MUFFINS

Very, very tempting if you are a chocoholic. You will need a greased muffin tin which fits in your oven.

MAKES	
about 10–12	

250g/9 oz self-raising flour
50g/1¾ oz cocoa powder
1 tsp baking powder
2 medium eggs
50g/1¾ oz light brown sugar
4 tbsp sunflower oil

250ml/9 fl oz milk
1 tsp grated orange rind
50g/1¾ oz dark chocolate chips
50g/1¾ oz white chocolate chips
Icing sugar, to sift

1   Remove the lid from the halogen oven, place the low rack inside the oven and replace the lid. Preheat the halogen oven to 190°C.

2   Sift the flour, cocoa powder and baking powder into a large bowl. Break the eggs into the flour and add the sugar, oil, milk, orange rind and the dark and white chocolate chips.

3   With a wooden spoon, lightly beat the ingredients together until they are just mixed (don't worry if the mixture is still a little lumpy – it is important not to over-mix). Spoon into the muffin tins. (Bake in batches if necessary.)

4   Put into the hot oven and cook for 12–15 minutes until risen and firm to the touch. Cool on a wire rack.

5   When cold, sift a little icing sugar on top of each muffin.

Gingerbread Biscuits

These are thicker and softer textured than the usual crisp ginger biscuits. Cut them into any shape using cutters or card templates. You will need an oiled baking tray with flour which fits in your oven.

SERVES 2–3

175g/6 oz self-raising flour
1½ tsp ground ginger
½ tsp ground cinnamon
55g/2 oz soft butter
1 tbsp golden syrup
85g/3 oz soft brown sugar

½ tsp bicarbonate of soda
1 small egg

To decorate
Glacé icing or melted chocolate and small sweets to decorate

1   Remove the lid from the halogen oven, place the low rack inside the oven and replace the lid. Preheat the halogen oven to 180°C.

2   Sift the flour, ginger and cinnamon into a mixing bowl. Break the egg into a teacup and lightly beat.

3   Melt the butter, golden syrup and sugar in a small bowl in the microwave – just for a second or two. Quickly stir in the bicarbonate of soda and pour into the flour mixture.

4   With a wooden spoon or mixer, lightly beat the ingredients together adding enough of the beaten egg to give a soft dough.

5   Turn onto a lightly floured surface and gently knead until smooth. Roll to a thickness of 5mm/¼ inch. Cut into rounds with a 6cm/2½ inch cutter, or use novelty biscuit cutters.

6   Cook in batches. Lift onto the baking tray, spaced apart. Put into the hot oven and cook for 10–15 minutes until golden.

7   Cool on a wire tray and decorate with the glacé icing or melted chocolate and small sweets.

INDEX